Doodlebug

A Road Trip Journal
by Robby Porter

Photos by Robby Porter and Louis Porter

© Robert Porter 2018

All Rights Reserved

Published in the United States of America

Bar Nothing Books
P. O. Box 35
Adamant, Vermont 05640

802-229-0691

info@barnothingbooks.com

Created with Bookalope

SAN 256–615X

ISBN print 978–0-9769422–2-1
ISBN Ebook 978–0-9987709–7-0

Library of Congress Control Number 2018900464

Table of Contents

Doodlebug..vi
Introduction..vii
January 1994 1
February 1994, 2nd month.. 110
March 1994 178
Epilogue 199

Doodlebug

The word doodlebug has multiple definitions. In Vermont, where I grew up, it means a homemade tractor assembled from parts of several other machines and usually used for logging. These contraptions are often ungainly miscreations that never quite fulfill the builder's intention.

Introduction

By the time I was 28, I'd driven across the country 10 times. All of these trips, except the first one, had a simple purpose: to get from one place to another—back and forth between college in Santa Fe and home in Vermont or out to Wyoming for a canoe trip or to California for a summer.

Because most of these trips were taken in an old Land Rover, which topped out at about 60 mph, I got in the habit going on back roads and avoiding the interstate highways. This imposed a perfect compromise between purpose and wanderlust. On the one hand, there was the necessity of getting to a destination; on the other hand, when you're winding around on two lane roads, you've already given up on getting there in a hurry. Sometimes it took six days to get from Santa Fe to Vermont, some-times nine.

The compromise meant that I got to see a lot of the country and I always knew why I was driving. Some of the happiest, most rewarding, and interesting days of my life were on those road trips. I had a variety of traveling companions—friends, girlfriends, my sister Molly, and, for the canoe trip, my brother Louis, who was 14 at the time, and our friend John.

At the end of the day, if a serendipitous turn brought us to a state park in a beautiful little canyon, I felt as though fortune was shining on me. The next morning there were more miles to roll away and another interesting stretch of road.

My first road trip was different. I was 18 and confused about what to do with my life. I had a vague idea, prompted by an article in *National Geographic*, that I would like to see West Texas, and no other purpose. I was scared, lonely, and miserable most of the trip. I probably should have thought more about that first trip before setting out with my brother on January 1 of 1994.

In the early fall of 1993, I started living in a rundown house on top of a hill in Middlesex, Vermont. It was a duplex with three bedrooms on either side and a rotating cast of housemates— former and future—and friends, lovers, and ex-lovers of all the above.

I felt at home with these misfits. I moved into one of the two empty rooms on what we called the "new" side, which wasn't quite as dilapidated as the old side. My housemate, Beth Ann, was a particularly charming woman starting a small business making and selling barrettes and hairpins. I worked for a friend and former resident of the house in his landscaping business. It was a good holding pattern but not really an answer for what to do with my life.

The way I remember it, Louis came over one day in November and suggested that we take a road trip.

He was 18 then, 10 years younger than me, but his argument had a persuasive logic: "You said some of the best times in your life were on road trips. What are you doing here? Raking leaves?" Somehow, a cross-country road trip seemed to answer this question. I was dimly aware that the trip and my life afterward would need some sort of purpose and so I decided to keep a journal.

It is hard to imagine now, 24 years later, but I kept my journal with an old Olivetti portable typewriter. Standing at the front of our truck, a 1979 two-wheel-drive Toyota Long Bed, and typing on the hood or sitting uncomfortably in the back, I pounded the typewriter keys into the ink ribbon and forced letters onto the paper. Today, as I sit here at my computer, the whole process seems as archaic and distant as the road trip itself.

I glanced through the journal occasionally over the intervening years. Most of the dog-eared pages were filled with complaints and pointless speculations, but there were parts that seemed bright and alive. I've cut out about half of the writing, added bridging words or sentences, and taken the liberty of reassembling and rearranging some sentences in ways that make more sense than the garbled constructions I wrote in the back of the truck. But I didn't add any content; what follows is all from the original journal. I did change the name of one guy who asked that I not use his real name.

He's dead now anyway, but I told him I wouldn't use his name and so I haven't.

Louis and I wandered, first going south to find warmer weather. Our route was determined partly by where we had free places to stay with family and friends and partly by whatever we wanted to see along the way. It took us a little more than two months get from Vermont to Los Angeles.

There was no perfect compromise for this trip. The purpose of the road trip was to take a road trip—sort of an existential tautology—and the pointlessness of it weighed on us from the beginning, as did the absurdity of a road trip being any more or less meaningful than any other endeavor—the typical existential dilemma. This sort of musing, alas, made up at least half of my journal. There were also interesting encounters and experiences and it's these I've tried to preserve.

January 1994

January 1st

We couldn't get a map in town because the bookstore was closed, so we figured we could just wing our way to Massachusetts.

It was a sunny day, the sky a ridiculous case of blue, but the road was covered with salty water and the passing cars, mostly in a hurry to get back to New York or Connecticut, left a fine spray hanging in the air. We ran out of windshield washer fluid and had to stop and swab the windshield with snow.

Took Route 125 over the Green Mountains, which are low where it crosses them, and headed down toward Middlebury looking for the Weybridge Cave, listed in Louis's cave book as being 1,200 feet deep. After a false start traveling down Cave Farm Road, we ended at the Morgan Horse Farm in Middlebury.

A man answered the door, puffy faced and barefooted.

"We need directions," Louis said.

"The Weybridge Cave? I don't know exactly where it is. You go up this road to the first crossroads, go east." He pointed west.

"You mean west?"

"Yeah, west, go west. Then there's a road called Hamilton Road. The cave is back behind there somewhere. North."

"He was asleep," Louis said as we left.

"Asleep, at 12:30?"

"Pilgrim, last night was New Year's Eve. His eyes are all bloodshot, probably got really hammered."

We knocked on the door of a house at the end of the road, a small dog barking in the side yard. A woman answered, peering fearfully through her screen, gaunt face, pretty but hard and hard worn.

"Looking for Weybridge Cave."

"Yep, it's right out back."

"Is it alright if we go out and take a look?"

"You've got to rope up if you're going to go down in it, otherwise you'll get in an accident."

"Can you go down at all without a rope?"

"You can go down a little way. Drive up this road and don't park in front of the neighbor's driveway or he will shoot you. Go across the bigger field and bear left; there's an oak tree and a little ravine."

"He doesn't mind us walking back there?"

"Don't block off his driveway."

The mouth itself was a small gash, out of place it seemed, an odd vacancy. Icicles hung around it and small ice crystals too. The hole was no more than three feet tall and less wide.

Louis went in first and I followed. It is a scary feeling descending into the unknown and reminds one of how pleasant it is to be alive, or how closely death is associated with the unknown.

I could hear the icicles Louis broke sliding on in front of him. Evidently, the cave sloped downward, and the sound of ice bouncing off subterranean passages was unsettling. I remembered the warning of the thin woman in the derelict house.

"It drops off right in front of me," Louis said and kept moving forward.

"Careful," I said, hoping he wouldn't think I was doubting his judgment, which is not exactly what I was doing but something close to it.

He leaned forward. "God, it is magnificent. Hand me your flashlight." I could picture him falling forward onto the jagged limestone.

In places it was not unlike an egg carton mattress, except harder and dirty. With two flashlights, Louis reported that it dropped off but he thought he could climb down, except he wanted to go out and rope up first. The cave was much too tight for any possibility of passing each other in the passage. We scrambled out, turning our hips sideways so they fit and trying to get traction on the broken ice on the floor.

I was surprised by how quickly and incautiously I went over the distance we had already traveled. The unknown is terrifying but the known is ignored. Louis went first and then I went down to the floor. Through a hole I could see another floor below, harder to reach—part of a small room with passageways leading off either end and round wet rocks on the bottom.

We were late to Alex and Vicki's house [Alex MacPhail—my parent's friend from when I was a child]. It is both inspiring and disillusioning to talk to Alex, my childhood hero. He has had adventures in the most unusual places; had dysentery in Afghanistan at 17, hitchhiked through Africa, lived in Europe for a year, walked across this country, and has taken great photos of it all. I am awed. Then I am ashamed by my own timid exploits.

Vermont's new seatbelt law goes into effect today. Another flake chipped from freedom for the greater good as defined by the insurance companies.

Jan. 2nd

We had a breakfast of grits. Alex and I were talking about butternut wood when the phone rang. Alex talked to his father and said he would drive up to New Hampshire to drive him to the hospital. I thought Alex would be frantic when he got off the phone, but he was all measured and calm and even tried to pick up the conversation where we left off. Apparently, his father has done this several times. Louis and I were edgy, wanting to get away and not wanting to hold them up. We made a hasty goodbye.

Missed Route 9 on the way out of UMass and fetched up on some unnumbered road. It took us to 202, a road that passes along the edge of the Quabbin Reservoir. A sign said Public Water Supply, No Trespassing. What a fine place to trespass; there would be no one else there to bother you. If I lived there, I'd hike in those woods anyway, camp there too.

Proceeded along two-lane Massachusetts roads. God, what a horror. Thoreau, where are you? Is your spirit here amongst these numerous oaks and occasional white pines? These are your roads, where you walked—no doubt passing horses and oxen. Now they are sheer hell. Endless towns punctuated by shopping malls, street lights, and traffic. The only freedom on roads like this comes from getting off them and onto the interstate, which we did, free to go in one direction and free to pass.

***

Tonight I heard several people on a television talk show arguing about the conservatives and the liberals. The difference, they were saying, is that liberals want to give power to a large government that will then administer freedoms fairly, whereas the conservatives want to leave the freedoms with the individual. I guess the liberals are responsible for the sign protecting the Quabbin Reservoir and a lot of conservatives drink that water, even in Massachusetts.

Jan. 3rd

We had just passed the East Killingly, Connecticut, post office when Louis spotted a doodlebug for sale beside the road. He squealed the brakes and turned to stop.

"Many more like that and we'll need new tires," I said.

"Come on," he replied.

Louis walked across the road to take a photo. Two men were framing up a small building on the back of a trailer. One of them came over. Probably in his late 50s, gray beard, short, round, yellow teeth with gaps between them. His shirt said "Dave" on one side and "Odd Jobs" on the other.

"What are you taking that picture for?"

Doodlebug

"See a lot of these up in Vermont. Didn't know you had them down here."

"I thought you were from the town. They've been giving me shit about this. Say I'm trying to sell an unlicensed wrecker."

"They call that a wrecker?"

"That's what they say."

"What do you call these down here? We call them doodlebugs up in Vermont."

"Just call it a woods buggy down here."

"It's an old army truck?" I pointed at the unmistakable five-pointed star, mostly rusted and rubbed off the door.

"Nineteen forty-one deuce and a half. You can put a cord of wood behind it if it isn't too muddy."

He pointed to a tree in the side yard. "Three tops like that and it will take them right out. We were using it last fall. Coming in after the loggers and taking the tops and selling firewood."

The woods buggy was long and heavy. A brown porcelain doorknob served in the door. Inside were old wasp nests and a few simple gauges. The dual wheels were taken off the back and the single that was left had chains on. A large piece of iron was welded and braced to make a boom and a cable ran from a winch out to the end.

"I had some guys from Providence looking at it. They're pretty interested. They restore old trucks. I guess they've got a good body but need a frame and running gear."

"So the town's giving you a hard time?"

"Yeah, they want their permit money is what it is. I thought you were from the town when I saw you get out with your camera. I wondered what the hell had happened. I thought, Jesus, they're coming in old clothes now. I'm used to seeing them in suits. It comes down to what your last name is in this town. The thing that bothers me, I don't own, I rent, and they send the damn letters to my landlord. He thinks it's funny as hell. I guess you have the right to sell something if you want to."

⁂

Made Hartford and stopped at Mark Twain's old house. It sits on a small knoll facing off some ugly, brick apartment buildings across the street and blocking Harriet Beecher Stowe's house. All in all it is an attractive house and rather imposing, although the press of modernity confines it.

We balked at the $6.50 price for an hour- long guided tour, but the cashier assured us it was worth the price, although she pointed out that she wasn't likely to say anything else. After we handed over the green, I overheard her discussing which tour guide we should get. "We'll get them a nice, sprightly, young one," I heard her say. The guide was young, not noticeably sprightly, but she had red hair, perhaps not unlike Twain's; maybe it helped her get the job.

The porch around the back of the house is magnificent—scrolled ends on all the rafters and in parts a complicated rafter pattern to accommodate the changing pitch of the roof caused by the round protrusion of a tower. A bench is built into a small bay in one section of the narrow part of the porch, and beyond the end of the house the porch extends into a large, roofed deck, perhaps 30 feet long and 25 feet wide, all of it surrounded by a pretty railing. It looks like a good place for people to gather in conversation on a muggy summer's day, and they did because the Clemenses loved to entertain.

It also looks like a good place for an irascible old man to watch his grandchildren, but Mark Twain wasn't that lucky.

He has no direct descendants. His seed, the seed of American greatness, carried only one generation beyond him. He outlived all but one of his three daughters and none of them had any children. His son died of diphtheria at two years old after a chilly sleigh ride with his father.

Inside, Mark Twain's house is splendid— fine tall ceilings, dark tropical wood, a marble floor in the entryway, lavishly carved mantelpieces and furniture. It feels cheerful and irreverent inside. They lived well on the money his wife's family made from coal mines.

He did most of his writing on the third floor in a room with a pool table and crossed pool cues stenciled on the ceiling. When guests came who he didn't want to see, he would hide out on one of the small third-floor porches until they left the house. Up here he worked on *Tom Sawyer, Huckleberry Finn, A Connecticut Yankee in King Arthur's Court,* Life *on the Mississippi, Roughing It,* and *The Prince and the Pauper.*

We left Twain's house worried that the trip would become a tourist tour. Rolled through New York, over the Hudson, and then over the Delaware River and into Pennsylvania, south along 209 through the Delaware Water Gap.

Considered camping for the night and I felt a little voice reminding me that it is foolish to hurry and foolish not to take risks, but we decided to push on to Max and Peggy's [our uncle and aunt] and avoid the snow.

Jan. 4th

We wake to rain thrown against the trees and windows. Every school in suburban Philadelphia is closed because of the weather. The roads, by Pennsylvania standards, are terrible.

We frittered the entire day away reading and playing chess, but tonight we are going to meet some people who work on a biodynamic farm/commune. The pressure is building on this trip. When will we be free? On the open road with no one expecting us and no one missing us. "Patience," my reason says, "nothing happens all at once." I can see that Louis is getting antsy. I suspect it is harder for him. At least I have the journal to write on.

The place is Camphill, a commune and farm school whose structure I can never entirely understand even after repeated questions. As far as

I can tell, the school we are going to visit is for handicapped people who are housed and live as though they were part of the community and as though they can overcome their handicaps, only more slowly than the rest of us. It is the inclusive philosophy of that old Austrian thinker Rudolf Steiner. Here two branches of his thinking have entwined, and Camphill is also structured around biodynamic farming, which is what, ostensibly, we want to learn about. Peggy sells her goat cheese at the Camphill store and knows Maria, who runs the store.

Maria invited us for supper, told us to park in front of the greenhouse and walk up to the garden cottage so we wouldn't get stuck on the hill. We expect a German woman but Maria is French. We expect plainness and somber humility in the face of mankind's notable ecological catastrophes and an acknowledgement of our role as gentle stewards. She is wearing cowboy boots, black jeans, and a sweater with a pattern. She is very tall and slender, mostly legs.

"We are looking for the garden cottage," I explain.

"Yes," she says holding the door open.

"Right here?"

"Yes," still holding the door open.

"I'm Robby," I explain as we walk in, still not sure whether this is actually the place or whether we have stumbled into a commune where the people always invite strangers in. Philip, her husband, is upstairs taking a shower. They live in this house with two intellectually disabled men.

For a few minutes we make awkward conversation and finally I ask Maria some questions about the farm. She leads us a little way through the house, introduces us to their two housemates, and opens a door. We stand on the steps, the warm house behind us—and it was very warm—with the door propped halfway open, looking out at the buildings in the light of the snow and the reflection from the town lights and the car lights off the cloud cover.

We stand for a long time talking. The cold of the night is refreshing and only slightly uncomfortable, but it eases us a little and gives us something in common, a small but shared suffering.

"Over there, see that dim light? That is the barn. The cow barn."

"What kind of cows?"

"Mmmm, mostly Brown Swiss, I think, but also Guernsey. And over there, at that house with those lights, the sheep farm. He has a lot of sheep, a great number, I don't know how many, but a lot. They get out in the summer."

Maria speaks with a bit of an accent but her English is very good.

We go inside and Philip comes down. He is very tall, even beside Maria, and like her he seems to be mostly legs. Dark, short hair and round glasses. With a jaunty walk, almost saucy, if someone six feet six inches tall could be saucy. Around his waist is a belt with a buckle in the shape of an American Indian chief's head and similar heads embossed all the way around the belt.

We sit for supper, boiled vegetables, meatloaf, corn, bread, and spinach salad. Maria puts Louis and me at opposite ends of the table. Philip asks one of the housemates if he wants to say grace and opens a book of prayers. "Take a short one," Philip says, flipping through it for him. "Here, read this right here." Philip taps forcefully on the page with his forefinger. The man reads in a nearly incomprehensible language. I was able to make out "Amen" right at the end.

Philip's accent is a good deal stronger than Maria's and he speaks a good deal faster as well. After listening to him, it is perfectly easy to understand Maria.

"Biodynamic farming is difficult to explain," he begins. "It is the more I know the less I can explain, and the more I explain the less I know. You understand?" He looked inquiringly at me but I know just what he means, although I fear that might be the end of the conversation. It isn't.

"The earth is a living thing, like you or me. Every part is connected to every other part. And it may be hard to believe but it is connected to the whole cosmos, the planets, the stars, and when one part is sick it hurts everything. You see, if I poke my hand," he picks up a fork and twists it toward his thumb, "I don't just say, 'Ouch,' here, but it hurts me all over."

According to Philip, the plants exist in a state of constant and reciprocal energy ex-change with the planets and the stars and a balance, which everything is accustomed to and which must be maintained for the health of everything, including the planets. Pollution, chemicals, radiation from satellites and radio towers, soil compaction, erosion, etc.—all deflect or inhibit this energy from reaching its intended and needed targets. Sometimes, the energy radiating from the earth is trapped and redirected back at the earth.

Philip speaks with passion. His sentences are short and fierce, accented heavily, and inflected for emphasis. The words come out too fast sometimes, and he makes a jumble of collapsing syllables. "Shit," he says curtly and backs up to start again.

He comes from the South of France, 15 minutes from the Mediterranean. There, his father is a "vinegrower," and Philip and Maria are going back there to take over the vineyard and practice biodynamic farming. They have 45 acres of vineyard.

"My father I can only work with for two days, three at the most. I say to him, 'Why do you do this or that?' And he just looks at me. 'Because my father did it and because his father did it.' Biodynamic. I can't talk to him at all."

Maria laughs. "Once we were there for three days. That's all. Philip put all our things in the car. 'Come on,' he said, 'we're leaving.' That's as long as he could stand it."

Near the vineyard he grew up on, his uncle has a large farm. But he needs bigger and big-ger tractors to plow because the soil is getting harder and harder. More burned, as Philip says.

To balance the plants and to put everything into proper biodynamic relationship with everything else, Philip prepares solutions of cow manure and other ingredients and buries it in a pit in the ground during the summer to collect the summer energy of the world. Then he sprays this on his plants. He makes another solution to harvest the winter energy out of crushed quartz rocks, and this he sprayed on the leaves of his fruit trees to great success this summer. The solution pulls in the light and runs out disease.

"How," I ask, "did anyone ever figure out all these preparations?" They seem so com-plicated. And yet, as Philip points out over and over again, you're dealing with invisible forces, like electricity.

"I would not try to work with electricity after only one day. You can't see electricity. You have to learn how to work with it. Otherwise, I would burn the house down or kill myself. It is the same. It is an invisible force. You can't know it right away. I think, though, after a while you get a feeling, so you just say it needs this or that. That's what I mean: the more I know the less I can explain. I learn from reading and from conferences and from people that come here."

I press on. "But how did they ever figure it out?"

Philip is always direct and never hedges on a difficult point. "By experiment. By trying different things."

Gradually, I begin to understand Philip. He is a scientist, a modern scientist trying to unravel the mysteries of plant growth. But more than that, he is trying to unravel the greatest mystery of all: why we have taken paradise, taken the Garden of Eden and despite our enormous ability to manipulate things apparently in our favor, why we have made such a hash of it all. Why are we threatening ourselves with extinction and pollution and starvation? The solution for Philip clearly doesn't lie in any solution that has been tried before because it hasn't worked. And so he is trying to divine what makes a good world.

This year, after two bad years, his apple crop was exceptional. Early in the season, he was out at 4:00

in the morning on certain days to spray a special solution on the trees, and he spent hours rubbing the bark of the trees to remove the loose flakes. "People think trees are all the same, but they are individuals, like you or me. You have to listen to the trees and hear what they say. Sometimes it is easy. I look at a branch and it goes like that," Philip makes a zig-zag with his hand. "I know the tree is saying, 'Oh, I had a hard time there.'"

"How do you know that your good apple crop was the result of what you did, or that it had some other cause?"

"It's true, other trees had good crops this year too. I look at the trees around and I see that they have many apples as well. But I look at mine and the fruit is bigger, more exceptional."

Maria looks bemused while Philip is lecturing on biodynamic farming. "He's the big chief," she says. But he says, "No, no. I know hardly anything." She adds little of her own about biodynamics except to go and get a book with a picture of an herb Philip is describing. But she seems to agree with everything he is saying, only to be less passionate about it.

I come to feel more and more sharply our rough-hewn Americanness. Philip and Maria seem to have a natural sense of manners and propriety about them. Not to mention their enormous height and graceful slenderness. I feel like some small woodland animal—scruffy, tough, snuffling around the borders of a forest, independent and wily but unrefined, while these two giants trade remarks with dignity. But it is to America they have come, and although they are going back to France, it is not without misgivings. There are 50 or 60 million people in France. The land is covered with people. Maria says that after the EEC [European Economic Community] and GATT [General Agreement on Tariffs and Trade] there is no way to make money as a small farmer and she thinks she will go to university and study to be an English teacher.

Near Philip's vineyard, development is curtailed by laws restricting where you can build on wooded land, but people simply burn the woods down and then in a few months houses start appearing. It is all under the table, says Philip.

I ask Philip if he really has any hope of improving the world by biodynamic farming.

If, he says, one piece of land is hurting then the whole earth hurts, but also when one piece gets better, that makes everything a little better. "It is very sick. I don't know. Of course, you have to be positive."

Some people say that they are going to make everything better. Philip thinks that the solution must start one person at a time, that it is foolish and wrong to think that biodynamics should address the whole world at once.

Perhaps, I suggest to Philip, we will run ourselves to extinction and other creatures will evolve to new places in the world. Philip does not agree. "I don't believe this evolution. You can think you come from a monkey or a turkey, but not me," he says. Philip thinks humans are the oldest pieces of the world. Probably they have not always existed in the same form but they have been here longer than anything else, because why else would they be more advanced and complicated than other creatures?

Philip, it seems, would be happy to talk about biodynamic farming all night, but Maria yawns and the clock verges closer to 9:00 than 8:30. I shift in my chair and wait to see if Philip or Maria move, but Philip plunges on undeterred. I wait a few minutes and try again—nothing.

I catch a pause. "Can we help you clean up?" I venture.

Philip's head jerks up and he bounces out of his chair.

"No, no, not here, you are my guests. In Europe, your guests don't clean up. That's not the way we do it. Here people say, 'Let me help.' They're doing the dishes." Philip shakes his head. "Not the way we do it in southern France.

"That must be hard. You have big meals in France, there are lots of dishes."

"No, no. No problem. In southern France, sometimes a man has two wives."

"You won't," says Maria.

We drive away refreshed, the night a gentle yellow from city lights reflecting off the snow, and as we turn, the cooling towers of Limerick nuclear power plant become visible, casting steam up into the night sky.

Jan. 5th

The day was a bust. After noon we left to drive to the Rodale Institute's test plots near Kutztown. We thought they would be an interesting and different perspective from Philip and Maria. Kutztown—and eastern Pennsylvania generally—seems to be what happens to a place when too many people crowd together in complete disorganization. Everywhere one person's enterprise clashes with someone else's in a battering cacophony of homes and farms and gas stations and malls and old shops and intersecting roads.

We gave ourselves a tour of some of the Rodale test plots and examined the remnants of unidentified crops protruding from the snow. It was savagely windy, but it felt good to be cold after being stuck inside for a day and a half. A researcher told us that during the winter they mostly crunch the numbers they have gathered from their plots during the summer. So much different than Philip? I wonder.

Uncle Perry [gearhead uncle who lives in California] called back to give us advice on the truck transmission. It has been rumbling when we decelerate, and the sound is particularly pronounced when going down a hill. By placing a whole, unfolded sheet of paper on the gear shift and holding it there with one finger, we can magnify the sound of the transmission until it is very plain to hear.

Perry's recommendation is that we drain some of the oil and mix a kind of paste, called assembly lube, in with the oil and then return the oil to the tranny. This paste is a thick lubricant used to make sure that freshly assembled engines and transmissions are lubricated when they first start up before their own lubrication systems have a chance to provide them with oil.

The problems are two. First, that we must mix this stuff with the oil ourselves, and that means draining and replacing it, And second, if we put too much in, it will clog the synchro rings and make the truck difficult to shift when the transmission is cold. Nevertheless, Perry thinks the rumble we hear almost certainly comes from a ball bearing. He thinks it will cure the problem and doubts whether it will ever fail completely.

Jan. 6th

I wake ambitious and fearless and suggest that we tackle the truck transmission. Louis agrees. We head for the auto parts store in Eagle to buy some assembly lube and spare 90wt oil. Our plan is straightforward: Warm the transmission by driving to get the assembly lube; drive home and drain the oil; mix half a tube of assembly lube in with the oil by hand, since Perry thinks it won't mix if we squirt it directly into the transmission housing; and return the oil to the transmission.

The parts store is set up on a similar plan as nearly every other parts store—several aisles of shelves full of automotive parts and additives and a counter the height of a bar bearing a couple of large parts books and a couple of computer terminals. We manage to locate the oil before one of the clerks offers to help.

"What are you looking for?"

"We need some 90wt and I was hoping to find one of those little pumps."

He came out from behind the counter to help us. A basic half-moon-shaped human, straight up the back, bulging toward the middle, with a trimmed gray beard that belonged in a western movie and a partly distinguished face betrayed by stupid eyes.

"No such thing."

"Are you sure? It's just a little pump to get the oil up and in when you can't, you know, get between the transmission housing and the floor of the truck."

"Nope. Doesn't exist. Got 90wt right there, no pump."

"I know I've seen it."

"Well, I've been in business for 17 years and I buy oil from seven different suppliers and I've never seen something like that."

"I know I've seen it."

"Yeah, where was that?"

"New Mexico, I think."

"Yeah, well, then you better go to New Mexico."

"I need assembly lube too."

"What's that?

"You use it when you're assembling an engine; it has molybdenum in it."

"He showed us a can of Slick 50 transmission additive. Louis and I studied it and he went back behind the counter.

"That's not what we want. Do you have assembly lube?"

The bearded loser had had enough of us. He turned to his comrade behind the counter, a small-faced, narrowed-eyed, balding scrap of intelligence.

"We got that assembly lube?

"What's that?"

The fool looked at me and I launched into the description again like a bad play.

"Manual transmission or automatic?"

"Manual."

"Aluminum housing or cast?"

"Aluminum."

"Try some STP."

"The advice I have is to use assembly lube."

"Well, I'm giving you different advice. Have to go a long way to find what you want."

"Thanks. Are there any other parts stores around here?"

"Yeah, right down Route 100."

In Pep Boys parts store we found 90wt with a pump and assembly lube. The only pump was designed to fit one brand of oil. It was a cheap brand and it wasn't the brand we wanted. We weren't out of the parking lot before I regretted this and wanted to buy the pump and take it back to the first store. I thought the chance to prove to an obnoxious asshole that he was incontrovertibly wrong was too rare and choice to pass up. Louis dissuaded me on the grounds that it was foolish, mean, and small-minded to be vindictive.

It was cold, perhaps 20 degrees when we got back to Max and Peggy's. We drove the front tires of the truck onto some boards to raise it so we could get under it easily. By the time I finished buttoning my special grease monkey shirt over the rest of my clothes, my fingers were too cold to work properly. Louis had to finish the last cuff button.

I headed for the house with the oil in a large metal basin, and Louis replaced and tightened the plug. Carefully, with my naked finger, I worked the assembly lube into a quart of new Castrol 90wt. I did this by cutting off the end of a large plastic ginger ale bottle and pouring some oil in it. Then I squeezed half the tube of assembly lube in. It resembled mouse shit in a tube — same color, same size (depending on the size of the mouse) and was no more pleasant to be dabbling in with my fingers. When it was all mixed, I poured it back into the quart bottle of 90wt.

We headed toward the truck feeling optimistic. Nothing to it, really, just hook the tube to the bottle, submit to a few minutes of discomfort lying on our backs staring up at the greasy, frozen truck belly, and squeeze the oil up and into the transmission. But the oil was too cold and the tube too long for the oil to pass through at any rate of speed, no matter how hard we squeezed. I noticed, however, that the tube was long enough to reach from the filler hole to the rubber boot around the stick shift. Louis pried the boot from around the shaft of the stick and I managed to force the tubing by. Once again, I thought success was right around the corner. We managed to force some of the oil through, but it took a long time, and once the pressure blasted the tubing off the end of the bottle and oil squirted all over the boot and the transmission mound and onto the truck floor.

Finally, in desperation we took the oil bottle to the house and warmed it in a bath of hot water. The metal basin we warmed directly on the woodstove. From here on out it was a siege which got progressively filthier and more obscene. Between bouts of warming the oil, we would rush back to the truck like two doctors in an organ-transplant operation. At least the hot oil kept our hands from being too cold. The tube itself was from an old bicycle pump—rubber on the inside with a woven jacket. The jacket, frayed and cloth, afforded much the best grip and resembled exactly the blood-soaked neck feathers of a beheaded chicken. As the misery of the job rose to ridiculous levels, it also became obvious that by persistence we would eventually get it. Louis and I got ecstatic and the quality of our observations deteriorated dramatically.

I feel a tension building between Louis and me. It is hard for anyone to be around me for very long because I am such a judgmental bastard and presume that my own judgments are of such importance to other people, which, of course, they are only to those people to whom I am important. Anyway, I feel there is bad blood building and I hope it will dissipate by morning. I think I have been inconsiderate and thoughtless about Louis's hopes and fears along this trip. I dole out my satisfactions and disappointments and expect him to ride with it without allowing him to have his own agenda and importance. And occasionally feeling this error, I try to create or instill an agenda for him, which, of course, only increases the problem.

Jan. 7th

A day of forced rest. The roads are terrible again, ice and more freezing rain. Why can't it just get cold or warm up?

We spend the morning clearing along a fencerow for Peggy. Louis and I wade in with machetes. It is fun work, almost cartoon-like at times. We swing in broad strokes as though vanquishing hordes of attackers. Half a dozen well-placed slashes and a large ball of vines is separated—top, bottom, and sides—ready to be kicked into the woods. It is violent work. The vines only have thorns for defense; it is enough to make them an opponent but no more, and we defeat them easily, for now at least. They'll be back in force next year. It is a wonder, a sad wonder, what pleasure one can take in ruthless destruction when it is authorized and sanctioned by someone else.

The rest of the day is spent in household tasks, mostly sharpening Peggy's knives. We do a passable job, given our small sharpening stones. I bake bread, we make pizza and do laundry, etc. All in all a pleasant day, but the itch to be moving on is growing.

Jan. 8th

Tonight I sit typing by candlelight, an entirely enjoyable circumstance occasioned by this damn ice storm. Max and Peggy's power went out around 10:30. Two hundred thousand people in the Delaware Valley lost their power today. Most of them lost it when ice-covered tree limbs broke and fell on power lines. We have the distinction of a sort of secondary cause. A power surge damaged the transformer that serves Max and Peggy's house. The actual malady is unknown, but Peggy's explanation is the most entertaining and has a sort of Aristotelian logic to it.

At the moment that Max and Peggy's power went out, their neighbors had a surge of power in their house. All of the lights in the neighbor's house blew out, the hot tub started whirling on its own, and their fax machine melted into a useless, foul-smelling piece of plastic. The neighbor,

Elizabeth, was drying her hair at the time and for a moment the hair dryer raced and sounded like a jet engine. They still have electricity in their house, but they have too much and it blows any lights they turn on. Peggy thinks that they are getting her power, as though somehow our electricity had been diverted to their house so they are getting twice as much.

Louis and I set out on our delayed foray into the Amish country west of here. Our plan, Louis's idea, is to park the truck and spend the day walking through the farmland.

I am feeling edgy and confined. There is freedom to the road, but you deprive yourself of it when people expect you home for supper and when you go on a foray instead of a trip. I don't begrudge it here. We are visiting, really, and can't expect to be free. But when we head out on one of these small expeditions it feels false, like a contrived line in a poem, as though we are trying to make chance happen to us.

I fear as we set out to walk that it will be a disappointing day, but suddenly a new feeling arises. We are walking, anything could happen. The walk itself has become a trip and anything that happens along the way will be a present. We are no longer looking for something but engaged in doing something ourselves, walking. Why this differs all of a sudden from driving, I'm not sure.

It is sunny and not terribly cold; probably the temperature was slightly below freezing, a pleasant day for a walk. The Old Leacock Road runs nearly north—south and we go south, away from Route 340. This is countryside thick with Amish farms. They are not beautiful to look at the way old Vermont farms are beautiful. Vermont farms are poetry, fragile against the rugged hills; painted barns and weathered houses are almost an adornment to the landscape. Such could not be said of the Amish farms; they look productive. In the shapes and colors of the buildings, industry rides above style, and as for fitting into the landscape, they are the landscape. Where one farms ends, another begins; perhaps some trees and a fencerow separate the two, but nothing more. The farms are not fitted in where the land permitted because here, as opposed to Vermont, the land is very generous, allowing itself to be farmed nearly everywhere.

It is not that the Amish farms aren't nice to look at, because they are. They are thick together without crowding each other. And one feels immediately the presence of people on the land, not as disconnected pieces using the land merely as a foundation for the houses, which are, in turn, a foundation for their beds, but of people who work where they live, whose lives are entwined with those of their neighbors.

Amish country

Amish buggies passed us going both directions. One passed, and inside a small child's face was pressed against the glass, bewildered eyes and a bonnet fleeting by. "That would have been a nice picture," I said to Louis. "Yeah, but I wouldn't feel right about that, forcing them to commit a sin or whatever it is for them to have their picture taken," he replied.

We walked on and saw two small children walking down the road toward us. Their mother probably told them to stay hard against the edge of the road, and here, where the wind had piled a small snowbank, they pushed against it, scraping their boots along as they tried to stay as far out of the road as possible. Each extended a hand in a shy wave and their small faces lit up with timid smiles.

I have always thought the Amish rather dour and hard-bitten people, but on this cold day they certainly appeared happy. Even the men, with their annoying beards shaved around their lips, grinned at us as they passed by.

We looked strange—two men walking down a small country road in the middle of winter, laughing and talking, Louis with a large coat and staff and me with a funny hat. I expected the Amish to seem irritated by us as well, but they didn't seem so. Numerous buggies passed us with women and children, old men or young men. They all waved and smiled, friendly. Three sleighs passed us with bells attached to the horse's harness that made a joyful ringing as the horse trotted. Behind one of the sleighs a small sleigh had been tied and several children rode in it.

We walked a giant loop, and as we returned the wind picked up. It turned into a bitter walk, heads down. Ahead we saw an old Amish man forcing his way against the wind to get his mail. His house was a rickety, wide clapboard ranch house, baby blue. It exuded bachelordom and had a sign behind the mailbox that said Tobacco Dust. He took his boots off on the porch, picked a broom from the corner and brushed off his snow tracks, and then went inside in his stocking feet.

Both of us needed to urinate, but we walked for at least a mile without finding a thick enough hedgerow to provide cover. When you can't find enough trees to take a leak behind, then that part of the world is definitely too full of people. Finally, we settled for under a bridge. Got home to find the power still out and the house slowly cooling down. Peggy made a wonderful supper on the woodstove.

Jan. 9th

Louis and I spent last night sleeping in front of the fireplace and waking every two hours to stoke the fire. What a marvelous way to spend a winter night. How many tired souls from days gone by flopped down in front of this large stone fireplace and eased their minds and bodies before its flames?

It went down to 10 or 15 degrees last night, but between the woodstove, the fireplace, and the kerosene heater, we kept the cold pretty well out of the house. Still, no work or sign from the power company and the dispatchers are as cagey as ever. They know nothing except how hard the crews are working and that they will get to us as soon as possible.

Louis and I played chess intermittently all day long. Overall, Louis is winning the bulk of the games. Our play follows the same pattern, time and time again. Louis catches me in a foolish, sloppy move and takes my queen or some less valuable piece. Thereafter, I play more carefully and I can play better with fewer piece anyway. Louis bludgeons me and I try to avoid him. Eventually, I succumb. Louis rarely makes a simple mistake but he has trouble arriving at a clean checkmate.

Then we went into town, or what passes for town—a huge shopping center—to buy groceries for supper. I find it so depressing that I almost fear for my sanity. Here are hundreds of mesmerized people staggering down the aisles under the weight of trivial needs and more trivial abilities, poked and prodded by the television screens blaring advertising from their suspended positions near the ceiling.

The checkout clerks seem to be entirely teenagers, mostly young men. Ours is dressed in the vestments of the store, dark turquoise vest with a name tag. His job requires almost no skill—simply pull the objects over the laser screen, pronounce a few repetitive sentences to the customers. His scornful attitude is betrayed by what looks to be a genuinely friendly face.

I feel superior and free as we drive away, and I stop instinctively before a yellow traffic light turns to red.

⁂

What are the main divisions between people? Max and Peggy say that how one behaves when things are difficult is one major distinction. Some people fall apart. Some buck up.

Jan. 10th

Power restored during the night. As it turns out, the neighbors were not getting our power, but there were two separate causes of power failure. Our problem was a blown fuse in the transformer which spared us the power surge that blew out the neighbor's power. Fortune and misfortune.

We set off on time and it felt good to be on the road. Stopped in Gettysburg at 10:30. Louis said it was a one-horse town, but it is slightly bigger than that — three-horse, maybe.

Outside, the roads and paths were covered in ice, so much that walking was difficult in places. We walked toward Little Round Top, which Louis thought was instrumental in the battle. Along the way, we passed a memorial to Vermont soldiers — several memorials, actually, the largest of which was to the cavalry. These soldiers held the top of

Little Round Top and down the back side to Taneytown Road, the back side of a key position, a fitting place for a Vermont group. Despite the ice, the battlefield enthralled us. We kept walking, long after we knew it was making us late for Charlottesville. Through the battlefields, past memorials where men like ourselves crouched and died. The absurdity of war. How could anyone march knowingly to their death simply to satisfy the plans of some general or the more distant plans of a president or Congress?

We climbed Little Round Top and inspected the battlefield below. It was, obviously, a great folly for the Confederates not to fortify this position, and once held by the Union, utter madness to think it could be taken. Below us lies the Devil's Den (so named by local people before the war), where Confederate sharp shooters hid and killed Union soldiers on top of Little Round Top. To their front, the Slaughter Pen, where hundreds of men died struggling over the rocks and brush, trying vainly — insanely, as it seems to us — to take Little Round Top. How easily the words of battle come to an inexperienced writer never a soldier — "taken," "fortified," "held" — the clear, solid terms of good writing.

From Charlottesville, Virginia, Louis called the Moores in nearby Free Union [cousin's of Louis's friends]. They said they were waiting to hear from us to know how many potatoes to put in the oven. We joked that perhaps they were vegetarians and started following their directions around and around on small, paved roads for quite a distance. Except for the fact that we had nowhere to turn around and passed no phones, I'm sure we wouldn't have kept going for so long, but eventually the road we were on, 601, intersected with 810, as Bill Moore told us it would. "Bear right at the fork and take the first drive after the wooden bridge."

The first drive was on the left and the first house on that drive was a small, red house with a dim light coming out of the windows and a Firebird parked in the front yard. A lanky, blond man appeared on the porch, dragging on a cigarette.

"Looking for Bill Moore."

"Don't know him."

"Said he lived on the first drive after the bridge; at least, that's what we thought he said."

"Don't know anybody around here by that name."

"Maybe farther up the road. Think they have a few horses."

"Nobody up this road by that name."

He must have decided that we were okay because he said, "I can call around and ask."

"That would be great, or we could just use your phone," Louis said, and the man led us inside.

The house was dark and carpeted in frayed carpet. A woodstove faced the door, burning a dull orange. A woman about my age was balancing a baby on her lap and the baby studied me with enormous eyes, wide spaced so it looked almost like a flying squirrel.

We were several hours later than we expected to the Moores' house which sits on a small knoll at the edge of a valley surrounded by steep mountains. Their house is very carefully fixed up. Judith did most of the work, putting down carpet and wallpaper with flowery designs and an elaborate pattern along the border near the ceiling. Around the house are several pieces of art by [Vermont artist] Woody Jackson. A small creek crosses the bottom of their driveway. Judith calls the crossing a ford, which may be correct; anyway, it is a word I have never heard a New Englander use referring to a spot in a stream in New England. But the mountains are very reminiscent of Vermont.

Bill Moore is thin with strong hands and a ponytail. He rock climbs, or did, and now he mountain bikes. He has his own business, a tree-trimming company. His face is angular and his skin seems stretched over it. He grew up all over because his father was in the service.

Judith looks like what I imagine a Virginia face to look like. Her mouth is expressive and always seems tinged with pain. She has auburn hair and wears it pulled back. Part of her family comes from England but she has spent almost her whole life in Virginia. When we asked her how long she had been there she said, "Forever."

They have six dogs: two Chihuahuas, a Doberman, a Chihuahua crossed with some-thing else, a beagle mutt, and a setter mutt. In addition, there is a small pig—half Vietnamese potbellied pig and half some type of wild boar. They expect the animal to grow to around 100 pounds and are hoping that it doesn't get much bigger, but they might be surprised.

"Well," said Bill, as we sat down to dinner, "we're vegetarians."

We are in the South, where language is naturally poetic. What a joy it is to hear these people speak. It is not that pronunciation is more beautiful, but the language is definitely prettier. Here, word choice is important not simply for content and clarity, but for style and drama. Southerners speak with natural punctuation—punctuation in speech and emphasis on emphasis. In the North, it is all clarity, brevity, and the beauty of logic. Here, it is delivery. The words themselves carry meaning, each word signifying something, even if taken together they prove nothing or say nothing original. They are a feast for the ear. The mind, perhaps, is left wanting, but the heart or the soul or whatever part of the human that savors beauty is satisfied. Bill Moore has a bit of this about him, more because he is a southerner than from any natural inclination, but nevertheless it is a pleasure to hear him talk, the accents fall just right, as a well-sung song with silly lyrics is still sweet to hear and so too is southern speech.

Jan. 11th

For Louis, lunch is an operation that often requires two hands. On the way to Monticello, Louis drove. We ate an early lunch because we were hungry, and Louis drove and ate and made me a good deal nervous. By his own admission, he is too inexperienced of a driver to do much besides listen to music when he drives; even carrying on a conversation he says is difficult for him. The road from Free Union to Charlottesville is very twisting; sometimes it is too narrow to have a middle line. I fixed him cheese and mustard on frozen bread, cutting and spreading on straightaways, holding condiments and food from flying off the seat on corners. In particularly bad sections, it is true, Louis put his sandwich down beside him and put both hands on the wheel. But when the road was straight or when he wanted to get the cap off his canteen, he steered with his knees.

What a place and what a man. It took Jefferson 40 years to build. Forty years he labored to make a place where he could live the way he wanted to. What drives a man like this? What force compels a man to such lengths? I don't buy the contemporary bullshit that he was so magnificently superior to the rest of us. No, I think here we must find inspiration more than awe, inspiration to be what he was in his finest moments.

    Our tour guide showed us the narrow staircases that lead to the upper two stories of the house, but we are forbidden to ascend per order of the fire marshal; two-foot-wide stairs with nine-inch risers don't meet the fire codes. So we descendants of Jefferson, living under a society he laid the structure for, children of frontiersmen, citizens, free thinkers, are protected from ourselves and have decided amongst ourselves that we better not lift our legs an extra inch on the stairs, and so we forgo the upstairs of Jefferson's house.

    Perhaps it is no great surprise that we revere Jefferson as a god of inimitable brilliance. We have taken such pains to shelter ourselves from the harsh world that shaped him—patrician, slave owner, but frontiersman also, playing in the woods, lifting his lean legs as far as needed for each hillock and rock. What did he learn on the edge of the wilderness? A respect for freedom and its consequences, faith in people's ability to judge for themselves? And now we can't go upstairs in his house for fear that some person will misjudge the stair.

Louis and I walked along the underground passageway that passes under Monticello and turns into two wings that run out perpendicular from the house. We passed the wine cellar where the famed dumb waiters descend from the living room, which I thought descended and somehow retrieved a bottle of wine on their own but which were actually loaded by a slave and sent on their return trip.

Louis's eyes lit up. "Pilgrim, there's wine in those bottles."

"You want some?"

"Yeah, man, you know how old that shit is? Look at this. Square nuts on the hinges. Give me two minutes with vise grips."

(Jefferson would have liked vise grips.)

"Edward Abbey would be proud of us."

"Get hammered on old Jeff's wine in his cellar. Once you got in there you could get behind a door and swill a couple of bottles down. Pass out behind the door until your feet stuck out and some tour guide saw you."

"The tour guides don't even come down here."

"The tourists would just think we were part of the exhibit."

What strikes me most about Jefferson is the raggedness of his life—the slaves and the Declaration of Independence, the extravagant house and life which he sold his books to partially pay for, the slave woman he had a long affair with who may have been his dead wife's half sister.

After Monticello, we drove into Charlottesville and to the U. of Virginia to see the section of it laid out by Jefferson. He imagined—I am fairly certain because the architecture speaks it so plainly and hopefully—the cream of Virginia's crop of young students (white men only, I suppose) standing under these columns, pausing in front of their dorms, gathered on the large porches and terraces of the Rotunda, exchanging ideas, questioning, wondering, pursuing knowledge.

We met a worker named Tom taking paint off the doorjambs with an electric paint remover. The wood of the doorjambs is old, original, possibly from the old growth forest of the East. You can see that the grain is very straight and parallel and there are practically no knots. Tom thought it might be maple but it looked like softwood to me, maybe pine.

"You know what I call this?" he said. "I call it the nerd line."

"The nerd line?"

"The best students, they get to stay here."

"Yeah?"

"You know, the honor students or whatever. They get to stay here. There are no bathrooms in these rooms."

"No bathrooms?"

"That's right. That's the privilege."

"Really?"

"Every morning you see them in their bathrobes. They walk out of the dorms and around the corner to where there is a bathroom."

I sat in one of the courtyards while Louis set off to explore the library. He returned in about an hour. He got lost in the stacks of Arabic books and had to ask for assistance finding his way out. It made him think that college might be worth going to after all.

On the way back to the Moores', we stopped to see Judith at the horse farm where she works. A flock of geese flew across the sky, their bodies just shapes against the lighter streaks of the sky, and nothing but honks when they passed across a dark cloud.

Judith squinted at the flock, looking for the one white farm goose that for three years she has been seeing with the flock of Canadians that live on the farm. She thinks the other geese consider the white goose special because it always seems to be in the middle of a group. This spring she saw a young goose that looked like a Canadian except that it had a white neck, so she thinks the goose is breeding with the others. It stays with the flock and flies north and returns every winter.

Jan. 12th

We wake to rain,
   "Listen to that shit," says Louis.
   "What?"
   "If it's raining like that here, it is probably snowing in the mountains of West Virginia."
   I took a shower and the drain stopped up. The Moores made us pancakes for breakfast. The Chihuahua Roy hopped eagerly onto my lap, gazed nervously into my face, and peed on my leg. It is a curious quality of some Chihuahuas that when they get excited, they pee. As for me, I knew it was time to leave.
   We gave Bill a ride in to Charlottesville and he told us about his early adulthood. He fell in love with a Norwegian exchange student during his senior year in high school. After he graduated, he

went to live with her in Norway. She was a city person and liked to spend her nights dancing and her days shopping. Bill liked to spend his time outside and he didn't dance or have enough money for shopping, but he was in love.

He had a job in a bakery and when his three-month visa was up, he got his employer to write a letter saying that he needed Bill to stay in the country. That was what he had been instructed to do by the Norwegian consulate in Philadelphia before he left, but it only seemed to hasten and harden the immigration authorities. He tried appeals. His father knew some people and he tried to pull strings, but it was all to no avail. On a rainy, overcast day, he left on a ship to sail for Denmark where his flight left from. The ship was full of old men and women, tourists jostling and carrying on as Bill tried to peer out a window and wave goodbye to his love.

Back in the United States, he took a job driving a forklift in a warehouse. His spirits sank, but he sent her a plane ticket to come visit for Christmas. She stayed for 10 days. Ten days of the most intense sex of his life, and he asked her to marry him and she agreed. Then she went back to Norway, and for a while they kept up strained letters and $200 phone calls. Gradually, it fell apart.

"She's probably fat and has 10 kids and I'm skinny and have six dogs, but someday I think it would be cool to go to Europe with my wife—to go to Norway and stop in and see her."

Bill advised us toward Route 33, saying that it was particularly beautiful, and perhaps he was right. All we saw were the shadowy forms of trees moving through the fog beside the road. They were beautiful, but we wished we could have seen out from the mountains we crossed: the Shenandoahs, the Blue Ridge, and the Alleghenies.

For $10 we get a plowed camping spot, a restroom with a heated shower, also a laundry room. The valley below us, the Canaan Valley, is the highest in the east—3300 feet on the valley floor—and these Allegheny Mountains used to be 35,000 feet tall.

Both of us are depressed tonight, I'm not sure why. Perhaps the mountains come too close together. We long for the West, where we won't feel the press of people confining us, looking at us from their narrow perspective. They say the West is conservative, but it is open too. There is enough space for people to be themselves, even if their neighbors don't approve.

I am unsure whether I am up for the writing task I have set for myself. But moreover, I am beginning to see my life as a failure. I'm 28 years old and living in the back of a truck, driving around the country. I suppose, like everything else, it depends on how you look at it. Every man I've talked to envies us. Perhaps no one can be happy unless their expectations are in line with their lives, and yet, for how many is that true? How many are happy?

Jan. 13th

This morning I finish off yesterday's journal entry while lying in my sleeping bag. Louis, upon waking, says, "I could write a great Edgar Allan Poe story. It would start, 'As I lay there, dreading the first strike of the venomous keys.'"

Journal entry
Canaan Valley

Eventually, Louis stirs himself to make tea, and after he makes tea he is inspired to make pancakes. I didn't expect that his small camping stove would be up to firing the large Dutch oven, but it does an admirable job. About 10:30 we set off in very good spirits.

We arrived at Peter Silitch's country house a little before 3:00. I was skeptical when he cautioned me about the roads and we had no problem with his hill, but that was our good fortune because it certainly was a tricky piece of road. For seven miles we drove along a narrow, paved road, only wide enough for one car. Fortunately, we didn't pass anyone else; if we had, one of us certainly would have had to pull over to the side. The paved road turned to one lane of muddy red dirt road and climbed precipitously. At the top, a small, ugly church stood at an intersection with no other buildings around. We turned right and then right again to Peter Silitch's driveway.

He greeted us on his porch. "Ah, here are my guests. No problem finding it? Good. Well now, what do you want to do? You like to hike, eh? Well, let me show you. If you walk up to the top of that ridge, there is a good view. Of course, it is a bit muddy; that's the problem with West Virginia. In Vermont, you have mud season, but here it is muddy all winter. If you go up that road there, the way you came, you can see over into the valley.

It is foggy today, that's the problem. I don't know how far you could see. It is supposed to get cold tomorrow and will probably clear. How long are you staying, anyway? Where are you headed from here? I tell you what—come in and we'll look at the map."

We followed him inside. Peter Silitch is a tall man with long, thin legs, small hands, and a protuberant potbelly. His face is curiously square. A few teeth are missing and it gives him the look of a jack-o'-lantern, an angular one. His hair is short and boyish.

He has a timber business and his office is in his country house. The house is shabby but sits well on the hill and is comfortable. He was in the process of doing his taxes, and catalogs were spread all over the floor.

"Look," he said, returning from another room with an aged Rand McNally map that bore the advertising of a local timber company across the front. "Now, how far south are you going to go? As far as Florida? I worked for a while in Dixie County there. Miami, now that's an Indian name. There's a Miami college in Ohio named for that same tribe."

"I didn't know the tribes ranged that far, all the way from Ohio to Florida," I said.

"Oh, yes. Those five tribes up in New York, they were like, well, like the Nazis or the Communists or something, only they were winning until the Europeans came. You see, they were warlike, but there is evidence that they supplanted a more civilized people who didn't roam as much. All across the Northeast, especially in Ohio, there are mounds. Mostly they think they are burial mounds, but nobody really knows. But they were a civilized people, maybe 2,000 or 3,000 years ago. Their civilization collapsed and they were replaced by these tribes of mostly nomads. All civilizations decline. Right now, our civilization is in decline.

"These Indians, the tribes of the Southwest, they had extensive roads and they had to go further and further for materials, then they succumbed. The same thing may happen to us. If the oil supply was shut off, the country would shut down in a matter of weeks — months, maybe."

Jan. 14th

We skipped breakfast and set out around 8:00 to see Peter Silitch's timber lot. It was blowing snow and cold. For several miles we followed him generally uphill and on unplowed roads that were slippery but passable. The Long Bed, which Louis was later to remark, "must have a monster set of brass balls," got marvelous traction for a two-wheel-drive, small-sized Toyota. Peter Silitch pulled over in front of a gas station and told us that he thought we should head on out of West Virginia right now or we might not be able to when the snow got worse and the temperature dropped.

We made for I-64 because we thought the road would be better than US 60. It was nearly clear in places and it always had a clear path of two tracks. Soon we were burning up the miles in a sprint against the weather. Our spirits crumbled again. Perhaps it is partly the feeling that we are running away from the weather or just running. Louis feels that the road trip is not what he thought it would be although he is not certain what is different, except that we are not seeing as much of the country and the people. I feel the same. Failure rides me, but from what? In two weeks, we have had a great number of good things.

I should make some notes about the changing topography. In West Virginia, the mountains were so tight and steep that Louis and I found them very oppressive. But as Peter Silitch pointed out, they grow very nice timber. The contrast between West Virginia timber and Vermont timber is starkly evident in winter. The bristle of leafless trees along a ridge top in West Virginia is noticeably taller than in Vermont, and one notices it with every glance at a mountain.

As the Alleghenies come down toward the east, the timber changes. The land looks drier and certainly it isn't as rugged. The elevations may be as great but the mountains don't have the stacked quality of West Virginia. Pine trees become a lot more common and farms appear sitting comfortably against mountainsides or in valleys.

I cannot say enough about how human construction and destruction alter the landscape. Not just in terms of resource depletion but in more subtle ways, the face of the land tells the story of the people. We live on land and what we build reflects our lives. Nowhere that I have seen is the land of this country in any large contiguous pieces entirely pleasing to look at.

Anywhere that nature has been left alone, the land is soothing to the eye. And in those places where humans have worked the land, loved it, cared for it, marked it with their lives and been willing to have it mark their lives, the land is, if not more beautiful than what nature creates, at least it is more inviting and peaceful.

Appomattox was a piece of road luck. We hadn't intended to go by it at all, or even given it a thought, but there it was. A shabby, leaning sign said

Welcome to Appomattox County, Where Our Nation was Reunited.

***

We saw the courthouse and the parlor where Lee and Grant exchanged letters. The house seemed less haunted than Gettysburg. Here two men came and sat together—two men probably more similar in their experiences in some ways than they ever would be or could be to anyone else in the world — and by quiet and dignified gestures ended an atrocity.

Lee rode for Richmond the next day with his son. How did he feel? Was it the same only worse than the crushing anger I feel when I lose a chess game after pulling it out for as long as possible? Was it totally different? Was he ashamed in front of his son? Was he ashamed for losing? For having taken so many lives? Or proud for having done his best?

Here we are, stopped in a motel in Petersburg, Virginia. It is costing us $33, and police cars and fire trucks are making a parade beyond our door. Louis sits eating canned fish steaks on his knife point and I'm snuffling through several cheese sandwiches. We feel like transients. The motel has maroon carpet, a pink bathroom, two televisions, and a king-sized bed. The Indian man at the desk suspects us of engaging in deviations here because he kept saying to me, "I treat you right, you treat me right. Keep it clean." I assure him we will, but that was before Louis started in on the fish steaks and pickles.

Jan. 15th

Two weeks in the trip. We are running from the weather a bit. It is pretty damn cold, although bearable. Drove largely on back roads today and saw some interesting farmland of southern Virginia. Seems like a relatively prosperous place although, with the exception of the Amish, we have yet to pass through a vibrant-looking rural community. Louis says that the South always looks slightly degenerate and worn down and that Roy Blount attributes this to the Celtic heritage of the people. Perhaps also it is the lingering effect of the Civil War.

We went to the edge of the Dismal Swamp and drove in to take a look. Once there, we decided to walk the four-and-a-half-mile road along one of the canals to the lake at the center. This canal, and presumably also the road beside it, was constructed under the guidance of George Washington and now is named in his memory. It was built with slave labor and must have been a horrible job, grubbing a canal out of a swamp. We wondered if there were slave bodies entombed under the roadway.

Our nine-mile walk left us sore and may have left me with some blisters on my feet, although I haven't bothered to look yet. I did discover my watch in my vest pocket, where it has been lost since the beginning of the trip, and so we clocked ourselves for one two-mile stretch at four miles an hour.

***

We are camped, if you can call it that, at the fishing access for Oregon Inlet on the Outer Banks.

Jan. 16th

I woke in the middle of the night with a tremendous thirst, the result of eating almost two packages of Ritz crackers for supper. We were out of water and the wretched Del Monte fruit-blend pineapple-grapefruit juice was frozen solid. It tasted like sweet vomit anyway. I found one water bottle with about a swallow of ice in the bottom and put it in my sleeping bag and went back to sleep.

 I dreamed a synthetic dream of Edward Abbey in Alex's house. I remember thinking that it was odd to be seeing ol' Ed since he was supposed to be dead, but he would probably think it was a good joke anyway. I woke and drank the melted water. Outside, a cat came up to the truck and started mewing. I opened the back and at the same time tried to wake Louis. Poor cat, freezing to death on this arctic night. By the time I got the back open, it was gone, although I called "kitty, kitty" into the wind for as long as I could stand it. I wasn't sorry not to have to pull some furry, flea-bitten ball into our truck, but I didn't want it to freeze either.

Louis never woke, despite the wind howling into the truck. I woke half an hour later and the cat was back. This time, I got the truck open fast enough to see a calico fleeing toward one of the buildings. I think it was looking for something other than warmth, like another cat, and was horrified to have some tramp in the back of a truck calling to it.

The road toward Hatteras was beautiful and deserted, which made it more beautiful and much more pleasant. I feel comfortable on any piece of land where there are no other people. I have never seen a piece of wild land I didn't find appealing. But there are many permutations from there to civilization. Few things are as uncomfortable as not being able to find your place on a piece of land, and this happens when there are too many people. The land itself always accepts you. You can always make your place, and if you make it well, then the land is more beautiful too.

From the New York Times—Temperature dropped to three degrees in Central Park, two degrees shy of a 100-year-old record. James Milcen, "It's not too bad. I'd rather sleep in a cardboard box than a shelter. I'd rather have a place of my own, but this box is fine."

About 1:30 we stopped at Goose Creek State Park to make lunch. The forest is beautiful—towering pines with small, dark green shrubs, rhododendron, and others underneath. Just as we were starting to eat, a couple pulled up in a car and started suiting themselves in sweaters and snowsuits. We ignored each other awkwardly for a few minutes, then I saw that they were putting on binoculars. I hazarded a question about whether or not they were looking for birds.

"Yes," said the woman. "There are a few rare ones in here. Some rare woodpeckers."

"I saw the sign."

"The red-cockaded, we saw one several days ago. Haven't seen it since."

"Where are you all headed?" said the man, bending down to squint under the tailgate, but he still couldn't see the license plate.

"We're from Vermont. Heading south and west. Road tripping,"

"How far west?" asked the woman.

"Well, California eventually."

"Hurrah!" she said.

"Yeah, well, we can't wait to get out of this weather. It is really a little too cold for camping comfortably."

"Well, from Vermont, you're more acclimated to it than we are."

"I suppose we are."

"Our pipes froze last night," the man put in. "I had them wrapped in insulation, but the houses around here all sit up off the ground. When it gets down eight or ten and then doesn't get above freezing in the day, pipes freeze. We're not used to it. Last time it got this cold was in '89."

"I guess we're more used to it, but it makes cooking outside like this a pain," I said.

"We've done just what you're doing many times. Camped out on the road, just like that. Slept on top of the Grand Canyon one time and it was five below zero. Then we hiked down into the canyon. Every 1,000 feet you go down is like going 300 miles south. It is 6,000 feet deep."

By evening we were driving through Croatan National Forest. All the trees seem to be pines in various stages of regrowth from logging. We tried two or three roads unsuccessfully. We had hoped they would turn into forest service roads, but instead they turned into subdivisions. We are near the coast and the curse of human overpopulation thickens.

Finally, we found a decent logging road among some tight, new-growth pines. Several hundred yards from the main road it opened up a little and we camped. It was dusk and the moon halfway across the sky. Louis fired up the stove and heated our cans of chicken noodle soup and beef, which we augmented with spaghetti noodles. It made a sad, peaceful meal. We felt safe, but lonely. Two men in the middle of an endless pine forest eating soup and staring disconsolately at the sky. We talked—what else—women and took little stabs and slurps at our hot soup.

Jan. 17th

The pines were particularly beautiful in the morning; a thick thatch of needles lay reddish brown around their feet, and above this their trunks were blackened for a couple feet by a fire, then the trunks rose in soft, silent pink lines to the tops, where the needles held a gentle green in against the sky. Behind them the sky was red with some heavy, gray clouds. The view looked like a painting—all separate, distinct parts and colors but very much a

In the pines

whole. A convention of crows convened just beyond my sight. Occasionally I could hear their wings and always their loud conversation.

Louis cooked pancakes—jacks, as he calls them—initiating a conversation in which we refer to every object, including ourselves and each other, as jack. We got pancake batter all over the tailgate by the end of breakfast. I think someday a bear may attack the truck just to eat the tailgate while we lie helplessly inside and watch.

Apparently, we outlasted the cold weather—that or outdrove it. This morning was warmer than last night. My feet itch from three continuous days of sock wearing. Something inside the truck smells. Certainly it is either Louis or me. Louis says the smell reminds him of the bear he saw in the woods at home. Whether it is body odor or clothes odor is hard to say. I changed my clothes this morning. Louis's have been on for a while and he has pancake batter spilled down his pant leg.

Got to Charleston. Bob Black [childhood friend of our father, now a lawyer] gave us a tour of the city. There are beautiful houses here. Before the Civil War, Charleston was second in size to New York and but for the war might have become a major port. It is still the second largest port in the South — a southern version of New York in arrested development.

Jan. 18th

Bob Black has had success in his case. The stay of appeal placed on his case by Justice Rehnquist was overturned by Rehnquist today. Camera teams and so-called news people descended in force on his office. We stopped in twice to say hello, but he was very busy.

We did get to see an interview, if that's what it could be called. The newswoman went over the questions with Bob beforehand and the entire interview was performed much more like a skit than any attempt to discover or explain anything. Amiability ruled, and when Bob forgot something he wanted to say, the camera and microphone were dutifully fished out again and he was let to say his piece.

The case itself is only marginally interesting. The Citadel, a bastion of good ol' boy military preparation, has been greedily feeding at the public trough but not permitting women to enroll. Senator Strom Thurmond attached a piece of legislation to some other bill, leaving this supposed loophole for The Citadel. Bob says it is clearly unconstitutional, but no one has challenged it yet. His client, a woman named Shannon Faulkner, craftily neglected to disclose her gender on her application and was accepted to the school, only to be rejected after it was discovered what gender she was. A stay was placed on appeals by the Supreme Court, but today the court reversed itself and Shannon will start classes on Thursday.

Seeing the newswoman interview Bob made me wish I had a profession. Her life seemed so much clearer than my own. She has a job to do and she can learn to do it well. She knows where she fits into society, whereas I can only seem to fit in as myself and seem unable to believe in a career long enough to make it a career.

Fleeing north out of Charleston, we stopped at Patriots Point to tour the ships displayed there, an aircraft carrier, the *Yorktown*, also a destroyer, a submarine, a cutter, and a merchant ship named the *Savannah*.

I have never before realized the extent, the sheer, absolute size of human ambition. Who, what ego thought to lay out such a project? Larger structures, larger single structures exist than the carrier. I'm sure there are more complicated ones as well, but for a basic display of complexity on an enormous scale, nothing I have ever seen rivals the carrier.

And so one stands on a deck looking up at a maze of wires and ducts, at a wall full of gauges and dials, at a floor full of airplanes, at fire equipment, radio equipment, gunnery equipment, navigation equipment, at an engine room connected to the bridge, and considers that the whole thing is wrapped in one steel hull, all of the pieces fit together and mostly watertight, shaped to ride through the waves and maneuver, and it is possible to see that all this is nothing more than a tremendous convergence of thoughts, different rational thoughts brought together in one impressive structure, one structure which represents—before math, before the black magic of hull design, before radios, before trajectory, before aeronautics—represents above all someone's conviction that all this thinking could be joined, peacefully joined if not for a peaceful purpose, into one coherent whole that would function and nearly carry out the intentions of its designers. Someone saw that all the different parts of thought could be united to perform together.

Thousands of minds created the ship, and what is almost frighteningly obvious when you walk through it is that no one mind, no 10 minds, could entirely understand it. It survives, it exists and functions only by virtue of cooperation. We paused midway into the engine room on a catwalk in the guts of the machine. "You'd almost think we could feed the poor," Louis said.

That's it, scholars, historians, political scientists, literature majors, and especially economists—the engineers have the day and they're taking it going away. Under fluorescent lights, with slide rules and calculators and pencils, with small nervous twitches and fearful, uptight attitudes that artists make fun of, the engineers have wedded the thoughts of many people into one impressive whole. It would perhaps not be so impressive nor so disturbing and dangerous if our thoughts about humanity and society and government and justice hadn't lagged so far behind. But here we are with angry people in the streets, a government no one takes seriously, and a warship so complicated it takes a community to build it and creates a community just to operate it, while on the drafting floor of society we are still trying to square the edges of ideas Thomas Jefferson laid down 200 years ago.

***

After a while we tired and went through the other ships. None, however, made much of an impression after the carrier, although we did ascend to the bow of the nuclear-powered merchant ship the *Savannah* and sat there for a long time, 80 or 100 feet above the water, just resting and enjoying the view and privacy since no one else came aboard at all. Louis looked at the ship and back to the aircraft carrier. "Wouldn't it be great to work on one of these? You know, looking at one of these ships makes me want a home."

Jan. 19th

We drove for miles down the west side of the Okefenokee Swamp, including a detour which took us slightly into Florida. There was road construction. The sign turner stopped us and then approached, walking very slowly and with a little wobble. There was an unmistakable southern menace in his walk, made all the more pronounced by the hooded sweatshirt he kept tightly around his face like a leper or a monk. He walked very slowly, like a bull that is determined to do something malicious just because it is a bull but is timid and slow because it is also a cow.

Louis crept the truck toward him, but he gave no indication of whether or not he actually meant to come up to us. Finally, he wavered near the hood. He scrutinized the license plate and decided to greet us. He had thought up his opener.

"You're a long way from home."

"Sure are."

"Where you goin'?"

"Road tripping."

So it went until we learned that he had never visited the swamp although he lived only 30 miles from it and thought it was probably worth visiting.

"He's never seen the swamp and 40 years ago he never would have been out of it," Louis said.

Pines, pines, pines. Another night of camping in the pines. Pines all the way from North Carolina to Florida.

Jan. 20th

Breakfast was grits. I forced down a cupful. Ugh. Why were they so good when Alex cooked them? We paid $14 for a tippy aluminum canoe and set out with no lunch since we didn't have any food ready to go and didn't want to take the time.

The Okefenokee looks a lot like a Vermont beaver pond, only with different trees and Spanish moss. Cypress trees surely rank with elms and beeches for beauty. Their shape is graceful and solid, from the buttressed roots and trunk to the vase-like top. They are a wonder to look at, even without needles.

We paddled for some time, a bit more than a mile, along the main canal and then turned off on the canoe trail, but already we had seen some sandhill cranes. The sound they make is partway between a bubbly cackle and a honk. The noise is pleasant but also wild and strange, jungle-like. We heard few other bird sounds, probably because of the coldness; it was about 40 degrees and damp.

The canoe trail was marked by posts tipped in white. Louis and I didn't feel any urge to abandon the trail and strike out on our own. Partly this was because we didn't see any other person or any real sign of other people, but also the trail felt very wild. Then too there was the fact that if we ever succeeded in getting thoroughly off the trail, and this might not have been easy since the swamp is thick and grassy, we might very well have never found our way back on. Our hands and feet were cold and so we paddled determinedly, passing through and jumping up so many cranes that we eventually got a little sick of them.

Four or five miles in we heard a loud splash behind us, which, for some reason, I thought must be a large turtle. I was in the back and when Louis turned around I saw the intensity on his face. Gator! I turned and saw a flat, black shiny nose and eyes. By this time, we had the boat moving backwards and I passed by the head as it submerged. When we got the canoe stopped, Louis was right over the spot where it had gone down and he began prodding around with his paddle. Suddenly, the water bubbled and an open mouth came out splashing water and flashing toward the paddle handle. Louis recoiled. Its snout just brushed his hand and felt, he said later, like a cow's nose, cold and hard. He thought at the time that he was going to lose his hand or more.

What happened next amazed me after I had a chance to reflect on it, although at the time it seemed perfectly natural, and that fact, actually, is part of what was so perplexing. We backed off and caught our breath and then paddled back to the spot where we first saw the gator. Apparently, when we first saw it, the gator was coming off a little island, and when it reached for Louis it was lying in the water below the island.

We started poking around with our paddles, holding them high up on the handles. For several minutes nothing happened; then it rushed Louis's paddle again. When it rushed, he realized that all the time it had been lying next to the island and he had thought it was just a log. This time we heard it hiss, a deep vibrating huff.

Now we had the sense to pull out the camera and I stirred for the gator while Louis tried to take pictures. It obliged with a couple more rushes and we switched positions. [We got only one blurry photo on the gator snapping, and a good clear one of it being still.]

While Louis was riling it for me, the gator seemed to get more angry—who could blame it?—and once rushed and rolled over on its side so we could see its white underbelly and tail. Louis saw its leg and foot, permanently crooked, short and thick, and thought

it was about six feet long. We were afraid now that it was very angry and might do something foolish, like getting in the boat. The thought of capsizing with the angry gator was too much and, after a few more prods, we gave up.

The swamp took on a completely different perspective. It seemed alive, absolutely fascinating, and every snag on the paddles or bump on the boat nearly sent us out of our skins. We very soon entered one of the most interesting sections of the trail—a cleared path with small trees pushing in on either side only two or three feet away.

This was a beautiful section of the trip, like a maze that kept unwinding in front of us. Occasionally, it opened into a grassy section and we could see large cypress or pine trees ahead. I had an unreasonable fear that an alligator might leap off one of the banks and into the boat. Once Louis spied some fur beside the bank. As we pulled up to it, the creature jumped into the water right in front of our canoe. For a moment I was sure it was a gator. Louis had seen that it was a beaver just before it jumped. He neglected to tell me and found my dismay amusing.

Tonight we are camped in the Osceola National Forest at the Ocean Lakes camp-ground. The

Okefenokee Overlook

campground is relatively unpopulated and primitive by campground standards (no showers) and only cost $6, which we were happy to pay for a place we could feel was our own for a night. Tall pines hung with Spanish moss, moonlight over the lake, a table to type on and eat from. No complaints.

Jan. 21st

I could no more complain about this morning than last evening. The sun rose flat over the water and made it a beautiful, dark, shimmering blue. The sky was fair and the light shone pink on the pine trunks. I heard the insane cackle of a pileated woodpecker, then I saw one flying with its irregular dropping stroke and knew, of course, that they come south for the winter. It was cool, like an early summer morning in Vermont. We stood still against the trees and let the sun warm us.

We are living somewhat like animals, satisfying hunger at the expense of being cold, a sense of belonging when we pay for a place to sleep against a sense of independence when we shift for ourselves. Coldness, hunger, and loneliness are constant companions—allies, maybe. They keep a load on us and keep us occupied either bearing them or alleviating them. Much satisfaction is gained this way, or at least some angst is deflected this way.

We boiled a pot of beans, black, and put them still hot into the kitchen drawer before setting out for Cedar Key. Twenty miles before Cedar Key we began seeing billboards advertising motels. The approach was anticlimactic because the map showed the key as an island, which it is, the farthest out of two small islands, but we crossed through some marshes and over a very small bridge and we were there.

We passed a wooden sign that said Homemade Arthritis Cure. It was in front of a ramshackle house which backed up on a little inlet. We stopped and knocked, and an old man answered. I shouted through the screen that we were interested in his medicine and asked if we could come in.

Inside his house was fiery hot. Books and papers piled everywhere. A blue, flowery sofa took up most of the left wall and faced a chair where he had been sitting. He pointed us to a framed article out of a *National Geographic*. The article was about Florida and had a brief piece about Cedar Key and a couple lines about him, Brooks Campbell. He was a boatbuilder, apparently, and he got arthritis and researched his own "cure."

"Now, you want to see something? I can show you things all day long," he said after telling us to sit down. He doddered up and returned with a jar containing three amber-colored lumps.

"Squeeze that a minute and tell me what you think it is."

We complied and guessed that it was some sort of pitch from a tree.

"That's kerosene and washing soda. My wife and I made those. Kneaded them up with our hands."

He pulled out a scrapbook of letters thanking him for his arthritis cure. I passed over one from the health department.

"They wanted to get me there. Thought they had me over a barrel, they did, but I knew about something, bribery, that's what. Yes sir, I know a lot of things. Could make a heap of trouble. You know all this drugs everybody's getting arrested over? Well, the government's growing some on an island."

"Really?"

"Yes sir. Now, I've got a pipe you smoke drugs in. You wanna see it?"

"A pipe, huh?"

"You wanna see it?"

"Yeah, sure." Louis and I looked at each other a little nervously as he walked away, but he returned in a minute.

"I got that when I was aboard the *Franklin*. For opium. You see, you put the opium cigarette right there." He pointed to the brass end of the pipe. It was pretty and long, fitted with a brass bowl and mouthpiece.

"I've got something else I'll show you. You wanna see a crucifixion made 1,000 years before Christ?"

"A crucifixion?"

"Yes, the crucifixion of Jesus Christ."

He returned with a small piece of bone about four inches long.

"Now, that's the skull of a catfish. Turn it over; you see there?" His large hands traced out the spread arms and feet and head.

We sat for a minute and then Mr. Campbell stirred again. "You wanna see my dancing boy? I said my boy—you wanna see him dance?"

He brought a small carved and jointed doll out of a drawer and a piece of a broken shingle. The shingle he put under his leg and tapped on it while he hung the puppet above it and the figure's wooden knees stepped in and out in a dance.

"Mahogany. Carved that out of mahogany 35 years ago. I carved those wheels on the wall too. Mahogany.

"I'm not a Christian, but I believe God put us here for a purpose."

"Is that right?"

"That's right. He has a purpose for us."

"That your purpose? To make medicine?"

"Yup, that's it, to help people. Now let me tell you something. You're young men, don't go out there killing things. Killing babies. That's not what God intended us for. I'm an old man and I know he put us here for a purpose, not for all this killing."

We thanked him for his advice and bought a bottle of his arthritis cure for Granny. Then we took another turn around the island before heading out. We were a little sorry to leave, especially Louis who thought he might like to stay. The first place he has felt that way.

Partway through the town of Chiefland we saw a sign for Manatee Springs State Park. Springs and a state park seemed inviting, so we stopped and decided to stay. Ten bucks a night, a bit steep, but it was early and we thought we could hike. The ranger said there were wild boars, alligators, and, occasionally, jaguarundi cats.

We camped and went to the spring, which was beautiful. It flows out into the Suwannee River. No alligators were visible and, clearly, swimming was permitted in the spring, but we lingered for a long time on the dock before jumping in. The flow out of the spring was strong and after jumping off the dock I had a hard time regaining it, even propelled, as I was, by the fear that some snack-happy gator was about to close on my feet.

We swam over the spring and tried to dive down in it. Once Louis thought he heard splashing downstream and we swam frantically for the shore, but it turned out to be a large fish.

A couple of people heard our splashing and came over. They were guest hosts, campground babysitters, who told us not to worry about alligators because they always stay down by the river and had never been seen up as far as the dock.

I asked if maybe in this cold weather they might not like to swim up into the spring, which stays at a constant 72 degrees, but they thought it unlikely. The fact that the manatees do exactly that and that one of the early explorers to the springs said it was crawling with reptiles weighed strongly against their assurances, as did their later comments that alligators were afraid of humans and swam away as soon as you got within 50 feet of them. But we swam and dived some more anyway.

***

After supper—beans we cooked this morning and rice, quite good—we went out to take a moonlit walk along the nature trail in hopes of seeing some wild hogs. Just out on the road we saw two flashlights running and passing through the woods, evidently circling in on some animal; we surreptitiously joined the pursuit ourselves. Then two boys dashed out of the woods and across the road. We came up behind them and they looked startled and then explained that they were trying to capture armadillos.

We, who had never seen a live armadillo, expressed an interest, and the four of us headed out down the road in the direction we were going anyway.

"You don't got armadillo in Vermont?"

"Nope."

"No armadillo?"

"It's too far north for them."

"Well you sure gotta see one. Last night they were all over. Saw a big old possum in that tree too. You got possum?"

"No possum."

"No possum? You oughta see one of them too."

We heard a noise in the bushes beside the road and all froze. "That's 'dillo," said the smaller boy, and they both flicked on their lights and dashed into the woods. Louis had his flashlight but I had left mine behind. We crashed through the woods for a couple hundred feet as fast as we could go, ducking and jumping over logs and undergrowth. Then we stopped and listened.

"That's him. Right there." Off again on the chase, but it was fruitless. The armadillo disappeared.

"Oh man. Last night there were thousands of them. They go under a tree and start digging. You reach down and grab them by the tail. Pull 'em right out. They throw dirt in your eyes, but don't worry about it. They won't hurt you or nothin' if you got 'em by the tail."

The little boy turned to the bigger one. "They can bite, though. Dave's got a big ol' scar on his thumb where he got bit."

Dave nodded. "Yeah, but they can't get you if you got 'em by the tail."

"You don't wanna get bit. He thought he might have rabies," added the smaller one.

"Yeah, but I didn't feel bad or nothin', so I just waited."

"Did you hear about the guy who died of rabies?"
"No, around here?"
"Yup, first person in 15 years."
"Really?"

"Yup. You hear about the dog that killed the little girl?"

"No."

"Doberman."

"A wild dog?"

"It was a family pet. Followed her right inside and killed her. Shhh, right over there, 'dillo."

We ran madly into the woods pursuing the poor creature. After a couple of hundred feet we stopped to listen for its clumsy running and then set off after it again. This one too eluded us, much to their disgust.

We walked back to the road, excited and focused on the hunt. Dave walked with a slight limp that will someday become a burly lumber. Already he was stout and his cheeks hung like slabs on either side of his nose, with two sharp eyes in-between. The smaller one had much the sharpest ears of any of us and almost always heard the armadillo first or heard some sound which he identified as either deer or 'dillo or hog. We made several unsuccessful pursuits and then turned back toward the campground.

"Saw a hog right here this morning."

"Really?"

"Lucky to see a hog."

"Saw five deer too."

Louis heard something way up ahead and we all rushed into the chase. As we dove into the woods,

I heard a grunt. "Hog" I called out, but Louis ran on. He stopped at a bunch of palmettos and started poking around with his stick. All of a sudden he came out of the bushes backward saying, "Hog."

Apparently, he hadn't heard me and had been following an armadillo when it disappeared into the palmetto bunch. When he poked into the bush, a hog went out one way and an armadillo the other. Our forces gathered we pursued it a little way then gave up.

The boys had to check in with their mother, so we turned onto the trail and walked along in the beautiful moonlight. The trees made crooked patterns on the ground with their irregular limbs. We made several more chases after armadillo and once after another hog, but to no avail. Then we took a walk down to the boardwalk and shone the flashlight to see the blue eyes of wolf spiders.

Jan. 22nd

The stove farted, surged, and wouldn't fry the jacks Louis tried to make. After pushing down several grease-soaked, doughy wads, he cleaned the jet and then it worked better—so much better that we burned the jacks. By the time breakfast was done, the dishes cleaned, and we were all packed and ready to go, it was 11:30. Stopped before Tallahassee and bought a bag of cheap pecans, which we cracked with our teeth and ate. I ate too many and now hate the thought of pecans. We stopped in the town of Blountstown and bought some bananas and orange juice to add to the concoction already working in our stomachs.

At the junction of 331, we get into an awkward moment. Louis says he wants to go on north [toward our grandmother, Muh's house] but doesn't mind staying. I say I would first go south to the Gulf, if it were up to me, but don't mind going north.

How does one sort out these questions? If we are both honest, we disagree about what we want.

If both of us are honest, then someone loses and either feelings get hurt or it becomes a tit-for-tat type of arrangement. On the other hand, if we deal in the nebulous land of each saying what we would like but never coming down hard for it, not only is it slightly dishonest, but then we are always second guessing each other.

We aimed north toward a national forest but were too tired, and so we stopped at a state campground. The gate said registered campers only, but it was open so we went in. Several empty slots among the

RVs. Louis backed toward the slab of asphalt sized for an American RV, missed it somehow, and tried again.

"You've got enough room on this side to land a 747," I said.

He looked hurt, pulled out, and tried again without saying anything.

Truck parked, Louis started to take a leak behind it.

"Jesus, pilgrim, you really shouldn't do that here. There are campers 100 feet away."

"All right. I'll go into the woods then.

The only happy thing is the wild geese down on the Alabama River. I feel like shit for telling Louis how to act. Life sucks. Louis goes to bed without supper. I eat a few bites of cold beans and rice. He reads and I try to sleep. Louis makes an overture of friendship by saying something about the possible Ranger Dick driving around in his truck. I know I should apologize but am not man enough. Sleep hard to find.

Jan. 23rd

We left around 7:00, pulling what Beth Ann would call a Bonnie and Clyde. Alabama land rolls and even has formations a homesick Vermonter might call hills. Hilly enough for us to hear the old growling in the Long Bed's transmission.

We saw a lot of big, open, and dry fields, a lot of roads deeply eroded into the red dirt, and a hell of a lot of logging. I think forest products must be one of the most important agricultural products in Alabama, but here they do not even have the dignity of logging in Vermont, and that is only the slight dignity of men against nature—sort of a brutal and short-sighted but at least romantic combat. Here the trees are reduced to lines and they are never allowed to grow to any significant size. Instead, they are snipped off full length and stacked on trucks like so many matchsticks.

Most of the Alabama towns we have driven through are preceded by a huge expanse of strip development. The town center is nearly evacuated. It is depressing to see those pretty old buildings, built by some generation which certainly thought it was passing on a legacy and history to its children,

Roadside lunch, Alabama

standing empty. Perhaps this is just the inevitable evolution, replacing the old with the new, toppling of the old trees to make way for the young growth, but there seems to be so much loss here.

The waste of the land strikes me even more forcefully than that of the small cities and towns. It is clear to anyone driving across this country that we have an abundance of land and are still an agricultural country. Even in these eastern states, fields and woodlots predominate the landscape. Where does everyone work and where does our wealth come from if we turn our backs on our land? And second, if we have stripped this land of its natural resources, as in the case of the forest we clearly have, is what we have built with this wealth going to sustain us? A third question is what ties a society together when it no longer has any connection to the ground it lives on? I noticed yesterday two sports stadiums — or perhaps one was on someone's jacket — the Seminoles and the Choctaws. So, when people need to choose a symbol to represent them, they turn to the Native Americans who preceded them on this land, but it is more deeply a connection to the land that is sought by naming their teams after the tribes that lived there. I find it hard to imagine a society completely separated from its land and even more hard to imagine an American society.

A bit south of Haleyville we saw a crowd of trucks, hot rods, and people gathering beside the gate to a drag track—Sunday afternoon drag racing. Several miles before, we had been passed by four fast motorcycles and these were here too. We stopped, and shortly the gate was open. This was not a race day; that will be in several weeks when they start charging admission. On this day, everyone was just having fun and a casual feeling pervaded the whole scene. Pickups raced cars, bikes raced each other, there was a profusion of smoking tires and squealing rubber.

The track was an eighth of a mile long and two cars would line up, usually after spinning their tires to warm up; sometimes they did this in a little trough in the pavement filled with a compound that got sticky when it heated up. A man standing between the two gave a signal by dropping both his arms at once, and they were off, occasionally with children or a girlfriend riding with them.

By 2:00 when we left, several hundred people had showed up. It must be an expensive pastime with tires and broken parts. We saw two cars blow radiators and such a great amount of rubber is laid on the track that it was entirely black and the pavement was buried in a coating of burned-on rubber.

Daddy says that when he was a boy, there were billboards on either side of Franklin County, Alabama, which said "Nigger don't let the sun set on your head in Franklin County."

Jan 24th

Started the day by heading out toward Russellville, Alabama, Muh's [our paternal grandmother] girlhood home. Muh's house was a sturdy-looking corner house. Her parents built it and she lived there until she married at 19, although she went away to college when she was just 16 or 17. We saw the sleeping-porch roof from which she jumped, using an umbrella as a parachute. Either she was an exceptionally springy child or the umbrella did slow her plummet a little. The roof must be at least 15 feet high and she did get hurt, although she didn't break anything.

Muh: "Louis do you remember when you and your mother came down here and the only thing we got into it over was the air conditioner?"

Louis: "Yes."

Muh: "Louis couldn't stand that air conditioning. He was always rolling the windows down."

Louis: "I hate air-conditioned air."

Robby: "How was it when you were a little girl? You didn't have air conditioners then, did you?"

Muh: "No. I don't know. It didn't bother me as much then. I don't remember it bothering me that much."

Robby: "How did you deal with the heat?"

Muh: "Oh, we'd sit out on the porches. Everybody would. It was better, really. Everybody would sit out on the porches and the children would play with each other."

We drove to the Dismals Canyon where Muh went on a grade school field trip. She says she carved her name into the rocks and trees all around the caves. Unfortunately for us someone bought the place, and was charging admission, all of which might have been tolerable since we had money, except the damn place was closed. Louis spotted a tear in the fence and Muh had no objection so we helped ourselves to the caves.

The caves, someone told us later, have species of trees growing in them that grow nowhere else this far south. Truthfully, it was cold and damp there and looked like the work of a glacier—huge rocks piled on top of each other making gloomy corridors and dank tunnels with high sides. In places there were great rifts in the ground. I wonder what ancient geological quirk made this strange place.

Then we drove to the site of LaGrange College and visited the grave of Dr. Kumpe. Most of the story is recorded on tape, but it pays to describe the countryside. The college sits on top of a hill. In fact, eventually all of the more well-off people from the surrounding land moved up onto the mountains, if not year-round then in the summer, because the weather was nicer. From the top of the hill we looked down on fields, mostly plowed and dark red/

black color, not unlike dried blood. The mud in the graveyard was sticky, red, and clung to our boots.

[Muh, from the tape]

He [Dr. Kumpe, whose grave we were visiting] was my grandfather's father. My grandfather was a judge in Moulton, and when Babe [Muh's aunt] was born — it was in 1889 — my grandfather wrote his father, wrote Dr. Kumpe, and said we have another baby girl at our house, and Mary [his wife] and the baby are tolerable. At the end of the letter, he said, "I'm enclosing a $20 bill because I know this is a bad time of the year for you." I thought that was so funny when we think of doctors, as we do now, making more money than anybody, but Babe said she guessed he got paid in hams and chickens and things like that and never kept any books.

A senator or congressman died and the governor of the state called and offered my grandfather the place. Babe said they were all so anxious to know whether he was going to accept it or not because it would mean moving to Washington. She said he would get up at 4:00 every morning, and this particular morning, the last day, he had to let them know whether he would accept it or not. She said they were at the breakfast table, all of them wanting to know and wouldn't ask him. Finally, he said, "Well, I've made my decision. I think I can do more good in Lawrence County than I can in Washington. I'm going to stay here."

He used to tell us the story about he was a little boy [in the Civil War] and the Yankees got after him and he lost his bedroom shoes when he ran from them.

They said a lawyer couldn't make a living in Lawrence County because Judge Kumpe [probate] settled all the disputes for everybody and took care of all the widows and their children and their estates and everything.

There's a woman in Florence [Alabama] who's really big on genealogy and all that stuff. She called me one day and asked me what I knew much about the Drake family. I said, "I know a good bit about the Kumpe family, my mother's people, but I don't know that much about the Drake family, my father's people."

"Well, you really should be ashamed," she said. "They were a very distinguished southern family. There's a bust in the courthouse [in Huntsville, Ala.] to John Drake and he is one of your ancestors. There is a Drake Cemetery where he is buried and some of your other ancestors are buried." So Jamie [Louis's and my cousin] was about 16 and sort of interested in that kind of thing. I said, "Let's go out to the cemetery and see if we can find some of your ancestors." So we did, and sure enough the first thing we saw was John Drake and buried next to him was so-and-so, concubine of John Drake. I said, "Jamie, I haven't found anything I'm very proud of yet, have you?" I'm not sure exactly what concubine means. I thought it was a mistress, but somebody said no, it was a second wife or a third wife or something, but I don't know.

Jan 25th

While at Muh's, the security guard, upon hearing that we were from Vermont, said, in a perfectly friendly voice, "Oh, real Yankees."

Jack's, according to Muh, had the best breakfast in town. Ours was mostly fried grease, tasty but not healthy. I haven't chewed anything in weeks—no, days. Some of the food we cook ourselves has to be well chewed before you can even attempt to swallow it. (Actually, some of the water we got from campgrounds in Florida tasted as though it needed to be chewed.)

We took Muh to her 9:45 doctor's appointment at 9:00, and at 10:30 the doc showed up; by 11:00 he was done with her and wanted to say hello to us. By this time, I had conceived a hatred for all of humanity. Dr. McCoy was a fat, amiable sort, somewhat envious of our trip but unlikely to ever take a similar one himself, although he had clearly thought about it since he mentioned that he thought it would be interesting to retrace the Lewis and Clark expedition.

***

We rolled shortly after noon. Went down the Natchez Trace Parkway that closely follows the old Natchez Trace trail. We passed some Indian mounds. The sign beside the mounds claimed that people were living in this area 10,000 years ago. Ten thousand years of sweating under the blank Mississippi skies, brushing through the leafy forests, treading the soft soil, and you start piling the dirt into flat topped mounds and worshipping around them.

***

Got to Clarksdale, Mississippi. John's cellar apartment, now also Molly's apartment, is one of a kind. Water is the dominant theme — water running down the drains from the bar upstairs, water dripping off the eaves outside, the dampness of the concrete, and, of course, the Sunflower River right outside his door. When we arrived, the main food in the refrigerator was a four-pound block of Parmesan cheese, a couple of boxes of soy milk, some chestnuts, and a few empty mustard jars. They seem to subsist mostly on raw oats and milk for breakfast, home fries, and occasionally homemade tortillas and cheese, obviously.

The Wesley Jefferson Blues Band came over to practice. It was a study in cultural diversity. The band mills with no apparent, at least to me, direction or organization. Beneath a constant conversation of mumbled words, whoops, occasional riffs on instruments, and nods and grunts, everyone seems to have some idea what everyone else is thinking or doing or about to do. It contrasts rather sharply with Louis and me and our spoken conversation defined mostly by words and logic.

Jan. 26th

John and Louis and I went for a walk around Clarksdale this morning. We passed the train depot where Muddy Waters boarded a train for Chicago in 1943. No longer in use. And past many other buildings that have declined and only been partially resurrected in one corner or one floor and then abandoned again and then revived again for some other purpose and then, like as not, abandoned again so a street archeologist could derive their histories from reading the signs.

John greeted and nodded to different people as we walked. Everyone seems to be a musician here.

Many of the buildings have been turned into juke joints. In front of one of these, we stopped to say hello to a friend of John's and then followed him inside.

Three or four men sat talking at a table and several more stood around in the back room. Decay seems to be the dominate theme in Clarksdale buildings. Even in the Delta Blues Museum, plaster has peeled off the ceiling. Here the walls were scarred, the ceiling patched and mismatched, the floor uneven and irregular. The pool table had been leveled by shimming its legs with boards. A general air of loose congeniality pervaded, washing over color barriers and even economic ones and rendering a feeling of ease and relaxation. Vigorous dialogue might be the most strenuous sport anyone engaged in. But violence, even death, felt as though it might be as casual and disinterested, as hopeless as fending off the inevitable decline of furniture and buildings.

Rain this evening too. Molly and I took a drive to Kroger and ran into her friend Panny Mayfield, and a friend of Panny's, who John says is a Jeffersonian farmer and a poet and a former politician.

Jan. 27th

Daybreak and rain. By noon, the water in the river is over low-lying trees, benches, and swing sets.

John's apartment leaks water into the bathroom and along the floor by the door and near John and Molly's bed.

Their bathroom facilities are unusual. There is running water in the bathroom for the toilet and cold only in the sink. For baths, John has made a sauna on a vacant piece of floor near the rear of the room, which is large—about 40 by 60 feet in size. He has bent some small pieces of cane into a dome over a piece of plywood. A tarp covers this frame, and both of the hot plates provide steam.

I squatted inside the sauna for a quarter of an hour today and got thoroughly steamed, especially on my upper body. My feet and legs hardly got washed at all, and I can't say that I mind. It got me thinking about bathing. Usually one bathes from head to foot and leaves feeling entirely clean, which is a good feeling, but, as I realized today, is rather one dimensional. Whereas cleaned by degrees, still dirty at the feet but cooked and steamed clean everywhere important, causes you to reflect and be almost physically aware that you are never perfectly clean, just as you are never perfectly happy or perfectly satisfied, but instead you are clean but a living organism that must not only be clean to be healthy, but also by definition is always in the process of getting dirty.

John has a stray neighborhood cat that moved into his place. He says the cat taught him a great lesson

John's cat

because she just moved in, and at first he was miffed at the intrusion into his territory. Then he saw that you shouldn't take more than you need and that the cat had seen this and simply moved into the unused portion of his space. Since then she has given birth to five kittens. I asked John if he was planning to get the cat spayed but he said, "No, why should I? There are too many people in the world, not too many cats."

Jan. 28th

Louis and I spent most of the day trying to gather pieces of piping and couplings to make a drain and run cold water to John and Molly's kitchen so they will not have to haul their dishes to the bathroom to clean them. This required trips to four different hardware and plumbing stores. Because the faucet John had was slightly unusual and fell beyond the range of what most clerks were accustomed to, they were unable to understand what we needed unless we held up the pieces and demonstrated.

Our problem was not that complicated. We had a sink and faucet and needed to attach them to the drain and cold-water feed. We tried to explain this to several clerks and the most impressing part of the entire episode was how inept most people are with language. After we assembled the rest of the parts, we were unable to get the water main shut off and had to delay the project until tomorrow.

This evening, Wesley was feverish and did not come to band rehearsal. Mike showed up and Iceman and Kevin and an unidentified older man. The rehearsal progressed in complete disorganization but with an underlying sense of understanding. After 15 or 20 minutes of conversation, mixed with small riffs and solos and tinkering with the equipment, everyone would come together on a song.

Mike tried to mold everyone else's playing to some inner vision of his own but was stymied at nearly every turn. Mike is a genius of some sort.

He is a brilliant guitar player, able to play any kind of music and seemingly able to hear what everyone else is playing while he plays. He sang occasionally and in between gestured to the other band members. Kevin, the bass player, is perhaps the best musician, quietly able to play anything and picking up behind everyone else, correcting Iceman on the drums and patiently staying out of the arguments, which mostly involve Mike trying to articulate his vision. John's electric organ covers all the open spaces in the music, like some sad blanket—a dolorous liquid filling every pore.

The only song sung all the way through by Mike was a version of "Frankie and Johnny," beautifully smooth and painful. Then he dropped into another song: "I got the surprise of my life. I saw my best friend's girlfriend kissing my wife."

Jan. 29th

We worked on the water in the morning. Had it hooked up by noon and then began trying to fix leaks. We considered just packing up and leaving instead of squatting under the sink. Molly and John would have thought this funny, at least after they got over their initial anger, and that almost justified it. Finally, we redid one of the PVC connections and got it fixed.

We left about 5:30 to drive up to Arkansas to see John's father, and on the way we stopped at an auction to stretch our legs.

"Who'll give me a dollar and a half, dollar and a half, dollar and a half, do I hear a dollar and a half? All right then, dollar, dollar and a quarter, do I hear a dollar and a quarter?"

Breaded chicken patties with cheese in the center. Six to a box. They went for $1.00 a box and one of the auctioneer's helpers distributed them to the buyers sitting in the crowded audience.

We sat at the counter and ordered coffee and popcorn.

"Do they sell other stuff or just food?" John asked.

"Other stuff—what do you mean?" said the woman behind the counter.

"Cars and trucks?"

"Cars and trucks?" She sounded incredulous.

"I don't know, cars and trucks or bikes ..."

"No. What do you want, snakes?"

"Snakes?"

"They had some dogs for sale earlier but you missed that."

Plastic bottles of lemonade-flavored drink went for $1.00, and packages of sausages went for $1.00, and we went out the door.

*
**

John's father is a funny man, one who doesn't seem to ever have been entirely settled and yet, at the same time, exudes a kind of peace. It is as though he keeps his discontent entirely to himself. He is a perplexing man, very gentle but neither unmasculine nor, I expect, entirely kind. He grew up in Vancouver in the winters and on his grandparents' farm in Alberta in the summers. Once he had a girl-friend in Alberta and he would hop freights and ride them from Vancouver to Alberta, including one stretch where he would have to ride through a 10-mile-long tunnel.

His father was a grocer in Vancouver. That was his life. He built the business up and spent all his time working there. During the Great Depression, he let people have food on credit. The people were families he had been serving for years and he couldn't turn them away just because they didn't have money. But he kept letting out more and more food on credit until he couldn't pay his own bills and, eventually, his own creditors came and took the business from him. It crushed him and he died a year afterward. John's father was 11 when this happened and remembers feeling as though he would have to take care of the family.

Jan. 30th

On our way to the Buffalo River, we passed by Blanchard Springs Caverns. Louis wanted to have a look, but a huge national forest building sat on top of the entrance. It cost $8.00 for an elevator ride 216 feet to the bottom of the cave, where you could walk along concrete pathways and admire the rock formations. We declined.

John asked the ranger at the desk for a map of the national forest, which she gave us. But when he asked if there were any undeveloped caves we could just hike to, she got suspicious. And when he pointed to a road and asked if it was open, she got even more unfriendly. To her, we were three funnily dressed people who didn't want to pay $8.00 to see her cave and who did want to go somewhere where there weren't other people telling them how to do things. To us, there was someone telling us how to do every little thing and some forest service building sitting on top of something we wanted to see.

No doubt the building exists for the protection of the people who might get hurt in the cave and possibly for the protection of the cave too, thoughtfully protecting us from ourselves and the world from us, like seat-belt laws. But who learns without mistakes, and what will the world be when there are rules for everything and everybody follows the rules? Will anyone learn anything? Will anyone have any reason to use their reason anymore? And from these unreasoning people, where will we find people to make rational laws?

***

Finally got to the Buffalo River and, after much rummaging in the truck, beat our way down an impossibly rocky and steep hillside to the river. We are near the edge of the Leatherwood Wilderness area and fairly close to the head of the river. From a cliff later we could see Buffalo City buildings in the distance. We camped in a small meadow and saw Osage orange and American hornbeam trees as well as cane on our way there.

The Buffalo River, what we saw of it, is lovely — green and sinuous, with curved cliffs flanking the bank. I caught up with Louis and John downstream, where they were just beginning to climb up over one of the sandstone cliffs. The stone made for unsafe handholds that often broke free. True to most hikes with John, we were soon in a position where a wrong move or bad luck would have meant death — in this case, by falling 50 or 60 feet onto the broken rocks at the cliff bottom. Louis came along last, John leading. There were several tricky spots where I feared the rock would give way and send me. I asked Louis if he wanted a hand but he declined, as I knew he would. One bald eagle soared below us and John spotted another upstream.

Supper of half-cooked bulgur with canned beans and cheese cut into them. Two cans of cold refried beans and pickles on the side. It is freezing or below. I went to sleep too close to the fire and had smoke in my throat for the first half of the night.

John likes rivers, Louis likes cliffs, and I like trees.

Jan. 31st

The hike back up to the truck warmed us nicely. We drove all day until about 2:00, when we got back to Clarksdale. John told us about the Mississippi—his favorite river and one he says is unlike any other in this country.

"A river is a very creative force. It is always looking for new ways to do things. Water doesn't like to flow in straight lines, even through sand, for more than 10 times the width of its stream. But around Natchez, the Army Corps of Engineers has made the river run straight for a long way, and now it is eating away at the bank on the Natchez side and houses are falling into the river."

Molly, Louis, John and I set out on the Mississippi from Friars Point. To Louis and me, the river looked a bit bigger than other rivers we have crossed on bridges, but bridges cross where rivers are narrow, especially when they cross the Mississippi. John promised us that this river would be different from any other, and he is right.

Molly and John and I were in the canoe, and Louis followed in the kayak. John figured that if we flipped, we would have five or ten minutes before the cold got us, not long enough to swim to shore in the fast current. Boils burst up beneath the boat and we crossed a dike submerged by the high water but still creating a tremendous amount of turbulence on top. We also passed some buoys pulled under by the current and deep water. They submerged and then rose out like whales, with a tremendous amount of dark blue water backing up behind them and a terrifying noise of rushing water all around.

The Mississippi is a moving ocean more than a river. The delta, the enormous floodplain, seems too large to have been created by the ribbon of water we passed over crossing into Helena, Arkansas. But from the canoe, everything is different. I had no trouble believing that the river was powerful enough to flatten 60 miles of ground to water-level flatness. The fact that it was 150 feet deep beneath us just added to my conviction.

The river boiled and ripped with eddies and whirlpools; it had undertows and currents within currents. Sometimes, the entire surface seemed to be covered in boils, great uplifting fountains 40 or 60 feet wide, spilling water from some torturous submarine depth into relative relief and recirculation. John said nobody is quite sure what makes boils, maybe some sort of release of pressure from the depths of the water.

The dikes installed by the Army Corps of Engineers keep the river in its channel and make horrendous currents where the river passes over them. Louis got so scared he felt sick to his stomach when he passed over them in the kayak. Life to me seemed no less precious than before, but I was aware how quickly it could pass away. We probably couldn't swim in the current over a dike, and in the main current, moving 10 miles an hour, three people can't right and bail a canoe in five or ten minutes. If we flipped, Louis in the kayak might have made it if he didn't die trying to save us, but then he would have to navigate the unknown river by himself and get to shore. If he went over, we might be able to save him.

On a map, the Mississippi looks like a meandering river rolling its way through bottomland and lazily turning corner after corner. But change in size eventually becomes change in kind. When the Mississippi turns a corner, a flowing stream of water a mile wide and a 150 feet deep slides into a sandy bank and is turned back on itself. Trillions of water molecules organized by gravity collide in mass confusion and purpose. A river, as John says, is always looking for something new to do.

Tonight we camped on a beautiful sandbar island. We walked along the upstream edge where the river is cutting down the bank. It is 100 feet shorter than last fall when John was out here. Our amusement was in stepping toward the edge and sending the cracked walls of sand tumbling toward the gulf—creative and destructive forces. I am bored except when I am making something.

February 1994, 2nd month

February 1st

Tugs going by all night. My shoulders and back hurt from sleeping on sand, but I was too lazy to brave the cold and scoop hollows for my hips and shoulders. Clear sunrise. At least an inch of ice formed in the water bottles. John seems in a foul temper this morning but pulls himself out of it quickly.

I am not happy to set off, not sad either. The knowledge that we can't swim more than 100 yards causes me to concentrate on balance. A tug pushing barges approaches downstream as we are passing by what John calls "some really wild water." We are in one of the narrowest parts of the river below Memphis. To myself, I lament the fact that we have two life jackets between the four of us. Louis is wearing one and John is sitting on the other. I am planning to use an Ensolite pad for floatation, if I have to.

The tug and barges are still a mile away, but John is already calculating which side of them to pass on. From where we sit—or rather, from where we slide along—the river curves around to the left in a huge oxbow. The barges are a mile dead ahead, maybe less, because we are closing quickly. Where we are, the river isn't much wider than a half a mile, but directly to our left is the point of land that creates the "really wild water," and beyond that the folded river stretches away for maybe a mile and a half.

Over there, in what seems to be flat, calm water safe from the barges, the current does strange things. It runs backwards, there may be whirlpools, and, more importantly, since we are in the channel, we couldn't get there anyway. Instead, we are going to stay with the fast water, going with the flow, sort of. The current will take us straight across to the other side and this is approximately what we want, or what John says we want, and our lives are entirely at his disposal now.

He is rather cheerful, but I can tell that he is concentrating very hard on things that still seem a long way off to me. We don't want to come too close to the opposite shore because the river moves like hell where it fetches up against the shore and it would tear us apart. Over there, somewhere, is another section of "wild water"— one John came close to swamping the canoe in, only that was in the summer.

If we were to go to the right of the barges, we would be closer to the shore, and proximity to land seems very dear to me right now, even if it is misplaced. But on the right, we would catch the full force of the thrust from the tug when it turned to take the corner. Already we can see the series of five-foot standing waves behind it.

The tug is pushing 36 barges upstream. Two buoys are between us and the barges. We plan to pass the first on the right side and then on the left side of the next and pass by the left side of the barge. John says to expect some rough water behind the barges.

When we pass the first buoy it is roaring, and five seconds after we are past it, I look back and it is just a harmless bobber disappearing and I know why John is always looking so far ahead.

The barge left us with rolling swells, easily manageable, like the concepts of infinity, meaning, and death. We stopped on another island further downstream and explored. Molly is planning to come back in the summer and spend a week painting, so I helped her build a crude rock fort. Then we went in safely.

The Wesley Jefferson Blues Band came over, and for an hour or so they were right on it. Gin was the drink of the early evening. Wesley poured himself a swallow from his brown bag and asked, "You drink?"

"Not much," I said.

"Well, you ain't missin' much."

John with the
Wesley Jefferson Blues Band

He has tried to stop many times himself, but he doesn't consider beer drinking, and after enough beers he starts drinking gin again.
Louis and I walked out to buy tequila when the gin ran out. John said to get a fifth and gave us $5. A school of stray dogs passed across the street in front of us, like multicolored apparitions in the neon lights. One caught its stride and, following

some nearly forgotten instinct, came back to cower, but seeing that we were neither going to kick it nor pat it turned back to the pack.

People hovered on all corners. Clarksdale is less peaceable at night, although a certain civility remains. It doesn't feel lawless, but the laws have nothing to do with legislation in Jackson. The hollowed-out buildings lose their possibilities by night and become hard and angry.

We bought tequila for Wesley at Goon's Grocery store. A wino tried to get 50¢ from us. "Sorry, man, can't do it," I told him, and we turned away and waited until he left, as though he might really believe our lie. The clerk, presumably Goon himself, was Korean and carded me. The wino came back in as we were leaving. "We're going to do it, man. Gonna have a bottle of wine tonight. Yes, sir," he said.

Feb. 2nd

Laura [Molly's friend] and Louis and I drove to Rowan Oak, William Faulkner's home, but it was closed for lunch. I wanted to see it and feel what a man fascinated by the unsolvable mysteries of the human heart looked at and presumably liked to look at every day when he woke up. I suppose I expected some tortured vines and gloom. Something of despair did lurk in the cedars lining the drive and the squarish house. "You see, it's not that big," Laura said. Perhaps the mystery was more in what inhabits a house after people leave than anything left by Faulkner.

***

Went to supper with John's friend Malcolm and Malcolm's friend David. Malcolm is a former state senator and farmer of wheat and soybeans. He has, in the terms of the delta, a very small farm of around 200 acres, which he inherited. As David pointed out, the land in the delta is always inherited because it is so expensive to buy.

We talked on a variety of topics, but eventually, inevitably, the conversation turned to the Civil War. The scars and memories lie not so deep. But what are they? Why does any serious conversation always turn to the war, if not directly then indirectly? Their resentment has cooled far beyond the point of being vicious toward us, but there is resentment for something these men did not experience and whose consequences to them have only been of the most vague kind. National pride, whatever that is, was affronted and has yet to heal. With a man of the soil like Malcolm, although by nature a forgiving and understanding man, there is an injury he can't forget.

"The South had chivalry and loyalty and manners and honor and, yes, we had slavery and lynchings," he says.

"You all eat grits up there?" asked David.

"We do some," I said.

"We don't eat them down here much. You go to a restaurant, you get them on the side of your plate," David said.

"We eat them more when we eat out than when we eat at home," put in Malcolm.

"You eat them with sugar and milk?" asked David.

"Yeah, I suppose."

"Down here we eat them with butter and salt. That's the way southerners eat them."

"Is that right?"

"Well, that's what they always say. I used to work for my uncle's little restaurant in San Antonio. He'd come in back and put sugar in his grits and then go out front and eat them with his friends. He never would let them know he ate them that way."

Malcolm was indignant. "He must have been infected some way."

"No."

"Must have. Must have gotten infected or been a carpetbagger."

Feb. 3rd

We said goodbye to John and Molly and took Route 61 south. Drove through more flat fields and occasionally passed by a catfish pond. I am simply amazed at the number of large tractors these farms support. Malcolm says the topsoil is or was five feet deep, the thickest, most fertile in the country, according to him, although an Ohioan might disagree. I guess the size of the fields and the richness of the land justifies, in some way, the tractors.

We stopped in the town of Gloster, Mississippi for gas. I asked the attendant how far it was to New Orleans. He was a young guy with an open, boyish face. "I don't know," he said and turned to a woman about his age who was walking by. "June, how far is it to New Orleans?" She gave Louis a quick once over and then said she didn't know either. "I'm sorry," the boy said, half smirking, "I don't know. I've never been there. I stay in Gloster myself."

We got to New Orleans at 6:30 and to Wilson's house about half an hour later. Louis navigated us without a wrong turn almost to the door, no small feat.

Feb. 4th

Morning began with a series of arguments with Wilson. He is a man who has dedicated his life to trying to make his city better through politics. He persists in believing this is possible in the face of unrestrained corruption. On one side, the argument can be framed by the simpleminded statement that you cannot have good food and music and also good government. That is, that the cultures which have excelled in entertainment and good living have not, generally speaking, excelled in just government.

After arguing for a while, we did go out to put fliers on people's windshields. This is an odious task, and Wilson made it worse by asking me to take off my hat so the security guard would be less likely to spot us and tell us to leave the parking lot. This request, of course, engendered another argument, and I left my hat on. In short order, the security guard did accost me and tell me to take the fliers off the windshields. I talked to him and refused until, eventually, he got tired and sought Wilson, who had been lurking in his car most of the while.

A brief and unpleasant conversation ensued in which Wilson tried unsuccessfully to explain to the guard how it is his right to distribute fliers in parking lots, even in privately owned parking lots used by the public, and that this right was protected by the Constitution and a Supreme Court decision stating that parking lots were the equivalent of Main Street 50 years ago. The guard said that he didn't care what the Supreme Court said, the owners of the parking lot didn't want a lot of useless paper discarded and blowing around.

I have to say that on the whole, I side with the security guard. Not only do I dislike the idea of telling people who to vote for in such a shallow and meaningless way, but I also don't like the idea of spreading pounds of useless paper over the parking lot.

In the afternoon, Louis and I walked by my old digs on Fontainebleau Street and then headed on a meandering course through Loyola and Tulane Universities. Both of us are sick to death of cities and hounding, pounding people looking at us, bothering us, pressing in on us, wondering why we are not like them, and generally being a fucking pain in the ass. Both of us want to be west and escape this miserable coastal clusterfuck as soon as possible.

However, I should say a few things about our walk. New Orleans has some damn fine-looking houses surrounded by especially healthy-looking vegetation. Today it was 70 degrees and drizzling. We enjoyed it thoroughly and could smell the city as we walked through it. Unfortunately, most of the time it smelled like a combination of sewage and exhaust, but occasionally we caught whiffs of flowers, perfume from a passing woman, food frying, and the pleasant smell of rain.

Feb. 5th

We met cousin Ousie [Perry's daughter] for lunch and had jambalaya and turtle soup. Ousie showed us a beautiful live oak tree whose limbs spread out and down to the ground so you could almost walk up on a limb and climb 20 feet into the tree and then turn to walk down another limb. It made me wish I lived in a tree house, or maybe even that several families shared one of these enormous trees and had houses in separate branches and a joint kitchen at the trunk. Ousie was somewhat miffed that no one seems to have a name for the big tree other than "The Big Tree."

Took in a piece of a Mardi Gras parade on the way back. I'm certain that I don't understand what all the fuss is about. Parades are mildly entertaining for a couple of minutes; after that, how many poorly played tubas does one want to hear competing with tractor motors and police sirens?

After supper we had another argument with Wilson about politics, then we tried to catch Ousie at the Buddy Guy concert at the House of Blues but missed her and walked Bourbon Street instead.

Feb. 6th

We began the morning by driving to get wood to repair the stairs at the back of Wilson's house. We bought pressure-treated, horrible stuff made from southern yellow pine and so green and wet that it felt freshly cut. Worked on Wilson's steps and went with Ousie to see the parade. She fixed us some nice food and then took us to exercise at the Tulane recreation center. It was good to have a bit of exercise.

Feb. 7th

Ousie picked us up at 10:30 to accompany her to her classes. We started with property law and an articulate professor explaining to us some of the intricacies of eminent domain. In particular, we focused on the price that would be paid by a willing buyer to a willing seller, and also a long discussion of how the government pays for land under a lease. The answer to this is fairly simple: They pay the owner the value of the land minus the value of the lease, which often leaves the owner pissed off since they get a price which they feel is substantially less than the property is worth. Apparently, they fail to realize that by leasing the property, they have sold part of it. It raises some interesting questions about what it really means to own property and whether using it or owning it is what really counts. Similar in some ways to the lesson taught to John by his cat.

Feb. 8th

I was tremendously depressed as we left New Orleans and I could see no reason and had no energy for continuing the trip. It seemed, frankly, impossible. I persisted feeling this way well past Baton Rouge. Louis was depressed also, although we wisely didn't talk about it until afterward. We tried to listen to music, but the best tape, Louis's mixtape with "Tangled Up In Blue" on it, had gotten tangled. He took it apart and tried patiently for about an hour to rewind the tape. He had to do this while we drove over a road with regular bumps, like small frost heaves. Eventually, his patience wore through, well beyond the point where we both knew it was futile. He crushed the tape into little plastic shards, and "Tangled Up In Blue," "Truckin'," "Take It Easy," among others, disappeared for us.

Somewhere beyond Lafayette, the land turned slightly western—that is to say, what the people have done or not done to the land turned slightly western. The farms were set back from the road, there were fields and only a few towns and houses. Also, we could see farther, partly because the interstate was elevated. The sky took on the look of an east Texas sky, ominous clouds above, lime-green fields beneath, but patches of blueness showing through clearly enough so we knew any storm would be swift to come and swift to leave. The vista was reduced to two main elements, open land and sky; for a while, people became an incidental curiosity. Our spirits raised immensely. We entered Texas happy and happy to be there. Only four states from the Pacific Ocean.

The Big Thicket is a national wilderness preserve, different from a national park in that oil and gas exploration and fishing, and perhaps some hunting, are permitted. We are allowed to camp without paying a fee as long as we sign in and out for hiking, a reasonable solution, and Louis and I feel comfortable here.

We hiked about three miles up Turkey Creek Trail through a variety of trees, pines, magnolias, and occasionally a beech. It is thick here. On the river, Louis saw a large snake slipping from a log into the water and another leaving the bank. It may have been a water moccasin and he may have fulfilled his lifelong obsession with seeing a poisonous snake, but we don't know. He did spot an anthill on the way back.

"Careful, those might be red ants," I cautioned.

"Not all red ants sting," he said, squatting beside it and unsheathing his magnifying glass.

"Careful, don't stir them up."

He bent over the hill, trying to get focused on an ant, putting his face and nose dangerously close to them. I watched nervously for signs of a war party advancing up my leg.

"Aha!" Louis said, sitting up and looking at his arm. "Great, I've got one on my arm. Yes, it has formic acid." He squinted at it with the glass.

"Does that mean they can sting?"

He prodded it with his finger. "Yes, there he goes. Have you ever noticed that some ants hunch up when they sting?"

"No, I never noticed that."

"They bite you and then hunch up because their formic acid is in their last section, so they have to hunch to spray it into the cut."

"Really?"

"Yup, look at that." He showed me the sting, slightly swollen and turning red, and he flicked the ant back onto the hill.

"Did you know that in some famous museum, I forget which one, there is a rare species of ant found by an English scientist? He found it while he was having supper with Stalin. It ran across the table, and he recognized it and put it in vodka."

"That works?" I said.

"The best, strongest alcohol will work. Now, army ants, I would like to see some of those. You know they can kill a deer?"

"No, I didn't know that. Do they live around here?"

"No, only in the tropics. Some of them are so specialized their jaws are only good for ripping and tearing. They can't feed themselves without the others."

It was about 70 degrees and breezy. I typed my journal entry in shirtsleeves.

Louis approached with a flashlight held beside his ear.

"Hey, Robby, wanna see wolf spiders?" I followed him and he shone the light around until he saw some eyes glowing blue. "All right, watch now."

We walked slowly and, as we got close, I saw a spider with a body about the size of a pea, but it disappeared quickly into its hole. Louis looked around and followed his flashlight beam down to some eyes. "Holy bejesus. That one is a meal in itself," he said. The spider was about the size of a grape. Its legs probably spanned an inch and three quarters, but it ducked into its hole and we couldn't prod it out with sticks.

"Do they bite?"

"I think so, but I don't think they are poisonous."

I went back to typing by lantern light. A few minutes later, Louis returned to the truck with an insect he had never seen before on a twig. It was about an inch and a half long and had large, grasshopper-style legs, but one was missing. He took it away from a wolf spider that had caught it and let it go, minus a leg, when he approached.

We decided to sleep in the truck instead of camping. This had the advantage of protecting us from ticks, mosquitoes, and snakes and spiders, not to mention ants.

Feb. 9th

Texas Flood. Louis and I sweated all night, and this morning Louis ate breakfast wearing only trousers. For breakfast, we had sourdough jacks and mayhaw jelly that we bought the day before from a roadside stand. The jelly was good, mostly sweet, without a distinct taste of its own. But the jacks were fine and we saved four for lunch.

By midmorning we were on the road and rain hit us, sometimes in downpours. The temperature dropped and the wind picked up. We left the Big Thicket behind and passed through many small, rundown-looking towns, ramshackle stores, and small, ill-kempt houses, yet somehow there is some kind of contentment here that I didn't feel in Mississippi.

Breakfast, Big Thicket

Austin was cold as hell. More than once we heard someone swear and exclaim about the weather as they passed on the street. By the time we located the University of Texas admissions office for an application for Louis, it was 4:30, and the office closed at 4:00. We had some bagels and cream cheese, whole wheat and seven grain, collegiate diversity.

Feb. 10th

Camped last night at Enchanted Rock State Natural Area. Freezing rain fell in the night. We heard it thumping onto the roof. This morning, the entire world was transformed into a crystal web of frozen grass and leaves and rocks. We hiked around the bottom of the Enchanted Rock. Prickly pear and yucca sprouted every-where, and all of this was set amidst a tumble of pink granite boulders and streams. It felt enchanted. Below us, the Hill Country stretched away, all laden with ice and beautiful, a diverse terrain clothed mostly in scrub oak. On top, 425 feet above the truck, the ice was still frozen, but on the lower half of the hill it was already thawing. Little rivulets of water ran everywhere, making a happy, lively sound. I wonder why no one put a homestead or cabin on this spot.

***

We stopped in Llano to buy gas and food, finally settling on a box of Grape Nuts, milk, two bananas, and a king-size Snickers bar, $6.20.

"That looks like a good breakfast," said the woman behind the counter, surprising me with a smile.

"It is, but a bit late for breakfast."

"We eat breakfast all the time."

"Yeah, I like breakfast myself."

"We often eat breakfast for supper."

"I guess I've done that a time or two."

I could live in Llano. It is a wide, sunny town and seems as though the people that live there know that it is their town. I could live in Mason too, the next town we passed through, with a huge town square and a main street almost four lanes wide—a western town.

The western Hill Country is full of wildlife. Altogether today we saw whitetail deer, mule deer, a roadrunner, hawks and buzzards, of course, a ring-tailed cat, a skunk, and many rabbits, both cottontail and jack.

Eventually, we found an open gate and drove quickly in, hoping that no one had seen us. We chose a camping site and parked, but both of us felt uneasy and so we decided to walk back out to the gate. It was a beautiful night for a walk, bright stars and juniper trees silhouetted against a violet Texas sky. I felt extremely uneasy and couldn't shake the feeling that something was watching us. Louis felt this way too and we walked no more than half a mile before we turned around and decided to leave. Who knows what makes a feeling like that?

We drove on, checking all the gates and turned away by padlocks on every one. If you want to pull off the road, you have to start looking at least an hour before dark. Eventually, we wandered off 377 onto a smaller road, 41, and then onto a still smaller one, 355. Here we quickly found unlocked gates, and Louis opened one and walked in to look for a campsite while I waited.

I saw his flashlight wagging off into the dark and I waited a minute or two. I was beginning to think that there must be a great spot when I heard his feet flapping and slapping onto the ground. He was running fast over loose, rocky ground. Then he came into view of the headlights and swung through the gate, quickly latching the chain behind him. "Jesus, I've just been attacked by a billy goat," he said. "You can't believe how scary it was. The damn thing came after me when I shone my light on it. I ran and then I couldn't see it anymore, but I could hear its bell tinkling behind me."

In a few more miles the road sloped steeply down to a river, and at the bottom we found another gate.

Louis opened it and waved me across dry, rock-strewn land under the shelter of some good-sized oaks. He made supper of bulgur, lentils, and tomato paste while I typed.

Supper was delicious, and afterward I went back to sitting in the front of the truck and writing while Louis cleaned up. He has a disconcerting habit of making loud, vehement exclamations and following them with no explanation.

"Shit," he shouted, walking up to the other side of the truck.

"What is it?" I asked.

"Oh my god," he said with disgust and started kicking at something on the ground.

"What's the matter?"

More kicking.

"Jesus."

"What is it?"

"Let's move the truck."

"Why? What's wrong?"

"A dead goat, right here."

By this time, I was out of the truck and around on his side. The goat was mostly skeleton and desiccated skin. I must have stepped right through it after I parked the truck the truck. Louis had done a pretty good job of scattering its bones with his feet. When he first stepped on it, he thought it was just an old rag. Under the harsh light of the flashlight, it was hard to see the bones among the rocks that covered the ground, but it just made them all the more eerie when we picked them out.

I started to back the truck to a spot away from the scene of death and Louis stood behind guiding with the flashlight. I had just parked when Louis got back in. 'They're all over; let's get out of here. I must have seen six or seven more and I didn't even look around. God, it was awful. It reminded me of *The Killing Fields*. I think they must have been poisoned. Their bodies are all contorted."

And to think that we had such a pleasant supper there and felt perfectly comfortable planning to sleep there. We set our sights on Garner State Park.

Feb. 11th

We skipped breakfast and walked to the Frio River. Slightly lighter than emerald green and flanked by large cypress trees. Then we hiked to the top of the ridge behind the campground, a steep cliff perhaps 700 feet above the river. Louis felt weak and tired, maybe lack of food, but he seems a bit listless generally. Things which would have excited him several weeks ago barely get a comment. From the ridgetop we could look down over the campground and river.

Louis says we may see 10,000 beautiful rivers and never stay long enough to know one. He is right.

The beautiful Frio River

I saw ravens making a nest in the cliffs and thought of how I would like to be making a place.

We left the park around 10:30. Nobody would have stopped us if we had driven right out, but I thought we should stop and pay, and pay we did—$16 for two rusty-water showers and a place to park. Hell, we could have had HBO for that much money. Louis was pissed and I can't say that I blame him. That's a lot of Long Bed food—a lot of food for us too. I felt bad about stealing from the park, possibly because I don't like to steal but also because it served us last night when we needed it. But $16 is ridiculous. Louis slammed the door, sighed, and drove silently, sulking, but he pulled out of it quickly. I had an urge to say something cheerful to try to make him act happy, but I held it.

We stopped in Leakey, Texas, bought some groceries, and lunched on our tortillas and cheese in front of the Leakey public library. One of the librarians in the tiny library told me that if I couldn't find what I was looking for in the card catalog, I should ask her because the library had been moved a year ago and not all the books were cataloged.

I found nothing on Coke Stevenson, [legendary governor of Texas], nothing written by Robert Caro, and so I asked her. We looked in the biography section but to no avail. There were no books on Stevenson and not even any bios of LBJ, although

I did notice many on JFK, which struck me as odd. We tried under Texas history and I found a short piece about Stevenson, but only about politics, nothing about the whereabouts of his ranch—the beautiful ranch on the south Llano described so vividly by Caro.

The librarian gave me another set of call numbers for U.S. history books, and while I was looking for them I spotted Caro's *Means of Ascent*. We hunched over the story of Coke Stevenson, reliving the American hero—solitary, honest, tough, fair, determined, successful, making his place on the landscape. Behind us I heard a man explaining to the librarian about the '48 election. That was the notorious U. S. Senate race where Lyndon Johnson beat Coke Stevenson by one vote, and in one county more dead people voted for Lyndon Johnson than live ones.

When I asked if we could copy the first 10 pages, the guy came up to the desk.

"You ever read this chapter about Coke Stevenson?" I asked him.

"Don't have to read it. We all lived through it down here. You ask anybody—well, my age or a little older—we all know about it."

"He makes it sound like Johnson stole the election."

"There was fraud on both sides."

"On both sides?" I was shocked and only partly concealed it.

"Oh yeah. It was politics."

"In this book, he makes Coke Stevenson sound like ... like he was incorruptible." I held up Caro's book.

"There was fraud on both sides."

"Really? I guess I'm sorry to hear that."

He pointed to the book. "Yeah, I guess he had to dress up his characters a little bit."

"I suppose writers do that."

"There was so much fraud. The Democratic commission investigated it for a long time but they decided there was so much fraud on both sides they gave it to Johnson."

"Well, we really wanted to see his ranch."

"His widow, Lady Bird, still lives there. I guess you can drive through. I'm originally from that country."

"No, I meant Stevenson's ranch. We want to take a look at his ranch. It sounds so beautiful in this book."

"Well, I don't know, but what you do, you go up there to Junction. Now, I don't know how it is up there, but down here all the old-timers gather in the drugstore. You go in there and you ask someone. Maybe somebody will tell you to go get lost but just ask someone else. Someone will make a phone call. Who knows, you might get taken out to see it."

"Thank you. Is there a charge for the copies?"

"No, anyone comes from Vermont and wants to know about Texas history, they can have them."

We tried a drugstore in Junction, but there were no old-timers hanging out. At the Kimble County Library, the librarian, Mrs. Murrs, said, "Well, you just missed his [Coke Stevenson's] wife, Teeney. She was in here over the noon hour. I saw that she had signed a book out."

We said we were going to drive out to Telegraph and see if we could go down and see the ranch. Mrs. Murrs said that if we got back before 4:00, we could follow her out to her ranch and see what a place really at the end of the road looked like.

Telegraph, Texas, is a store with a few houses, like two or three. The Stevenson ranch sits in the river canyon below, maybe a mile distant. The proprietor of the store looked a bit doubtful about our request but said she would call Teeney Stevenson and ask if we could come look at the ranch. Teeney said she was too busy, but the woman running the store opened up to us a bit.

"Where you all from?"

"We're from Vermont. We read about Coke Stevenson in a book, Caro's book."

"That's the one." She looked mildly dis-gusted.

"He made his ranch sound so beautiful we wanted to see it."

"You come all this way for that?"

"Well, no, we're taking a road trip all across the country."

"Well, I'll tell you. I knew him. I took care of him in his later years."

"Really?"

"I'm a registered nurse."

"Caro makes him out to be a hero in that book."

"Well, he was a politician."

"I guess that is what this fella down in Leakey was trying to tell us."

"Politics is politics."

"The book made him sound pretty honest."

"Well, he was a politician. He didn't even carry that election in this county, I don't think. People knew him here."

"What kind of person was he?"

"Radically conservative."

"Radically conservative? What do you mean?"

"You know what conservative means?"

"I think so."

"Chintzy."

"Really?"

"Yup, I don't know how he ran the state."

"I remember in the book where it said he always saved a little bit of every bit of money he made. Guess it depends on how you read it."

"I don't know how he ran the state. Kept track of every bit of money. You know these new inventions, computers and all? He was against all of it. They wanted to put a dam on the river. You saw the dam in town. He was against it."

"I guess it is good to hear both sides."

"Well, it's not both sides. He was a great man in some ways, I guess."

"The book made him sound like a hero."

"He was a politician."

We drove up to the top of the hill and looked down on what we could see of the ranch and the house Coke Stevenson built himself. It looked like a fine spot. A small river valley flanked by canyon walls on one side and on the other side the steep hill we were standing on—5,500 acres on that side and another 5,500 across the road, plus 3,000 downstream, split up now among his children but all part of the ranch when Coke was there.

Junction had a different look to me when we drove back into it. I could still live there, wide streets, people who meant to stay or were so far away from the mainstream that it didn't pull them into its discontent. But the luster was gone, disillusioned.

We followed Mrs. Murrs home and learned what it means to live on the end of the road in Texas. It means stream crossings and cattle guards and miles of dirt roads. The Long Bed is a valiant road warrior but Mrs. Murrs's big Ford definitely had more water clearance fording streams.

We met her husband, Horsefly, who has enormous hands swollen from work outside and a Texas face shaped by winds, grins, and squints. Also met their grandchildren Chris, Chad, and Matt, all shy and friendly.

Mrs. Murrs read from our copy of Caro. She read firmly and pronounced decisively, reminding me of a time when we weren't so inundated with words, so when people read, they looked for the meaning in each sentence because if someone was going to the bother of writing, they must have had something meaningful to say.

In all the vast and empty Hill Country, there was no more deserted area than the seventy miles of rolling hills and towering limestone cliffs between Brady and Junction, about eighty miles west of Johnson City. Only a few widely scattered ranch houses dotted that area; for long stretches, after night fell, not a single light marked a human presence. Beginning in the year 1904, however, there was one light. It was the light of a campfire. Each night it was in a different location, for it marked the camp of a wagon traveling back and forth between Brady and Junction. Lying in the little circle of flickering light cast by the fire was a single person: a slender teenage boy. He would be lying beside the fire on his stomach, reading a book.

The boy was the son of impoverished parents. He was determined to be something more, and his determination had led him to haul freight between Junction and Brady. Older men, deterred by the loneliness of the five nights alone each week in the trackless hills and by the seven dangerous, often impassable, streams that would have to be forded on each trip, had refused to even try to do that.

—Robert Caro, Means of Ascent, chapter eight, "The Story of Coke Stevenson"

We all pored over the map, trying to figure where Stevenson's freight route was.

"Well, I don't see how you can get seven river crossings out of that, except maybe he was reading those law books and no telling where he was going. Might not have been watching that carefully. Probably went up through London and Cow Creek," said Mr. Murrs.

"We thought he was kind of a hero," I said.

"I guess he was, but he was a politician, you know. That ranch he got from Old Man Flemings. Flemings killed someone and Coke got him off and ended up with the ranch."

The Murrs offered us a place to camp and invited us to breakfast. Mr. Murrs walked us out on their land. It is unbelievably rocky, even to a Vermonter. "You can go a mile in that direction, a mile that way, and a mile and a half that way," he said. Typing tonight by juniper campfire, romantic and aromatic.

Feb. 12th

For days now, Louis has had a hankering for biscuits, and so we were very pleasantly surprised when Mrs. Murrs said, "It'll be a few minutes; the biscuits aren't quite done." Biscuits with butter and honey, jelly, bacon, and a big bowl of scrambled eggs, chairs and a table, no wind—opulence. We talked and told stories and felt at ease. Then we left, back across ten cattle guards, three creek fordings, and six miles of rough road.

Took a possible Coke Stevenson wagon route from Junction up to Brady. We counted five stream crossings, two of them dry. That might make seven if he had to cross the Llano twice on the way into Junction, which Louis thinks was the case. The terrain didn't look all that rugged to us. It had some rough spots, but generally the country seems more rugged south of Junction than north and east.

I am more impressed by the awful loneliness he must have endured. I have been a little lonely myself. Even with the two of us, sometimes the winter nights seem to last forever and I wake over and over again looking for the dawn. How hard it must have been for him night after night with no one but the horses. So hard, according to Caro, that Stevenson didn't talk about the freighting days until years afterward.

And he was driven by what? All to secure a place for himself, night after night under the wagon, just to scrape together the money to buy a piece of land where he wanted to live in the piece of the world he felt he belonged to. I remembered what the woman in the store in Telegraph said: "He didn't sleep much. Not like you or me. He was always up around 3:00. Who knows — maybe he went to bed with the chickens, but he didn't sleep straight through like you or me."

From Brady, we turned back west on 190 through Mulligan Draw, Poor Hollow, Buck-horn Draw, just to name the ones I remember. The country here turned flat and by its flatness even less hospitable than the stony ground around the Murrses' ranch. On the long, barren stretch between Menard and Iraan, everybody we passed waved at us, not, obviously, because they knew us but because we were other people.

We pulled off onto a dirt road south of Fort Stockton and then down another until we found what seemed to be a suitable spot. Went for a hike in the hills, or foothills to the mountains. What a happy sight are mountains to these Vermonters. Louis loves this land, while he was very sick of the flat land 40 miles ago.

    Tonight we are living like cowboys, minus the horses and cows. Louis tried to start his stove, but for the first time it failed us and would only run at half speed, so we cooked over the campfire. Mrs. Murrs sent us off with two half pound venison and pork sausages, some tortillas, and raisin bread. Sausages were lean and fine. Parked in the desert, eating and typing from the campfire, as free on the range as one can be now that it is fenced.

The Longbed in the Glass Mountains

I thought of poor old Ed Abbey as we bedded down. The loneliness and the feeling of trespassing made me think of how he relished such nights and drew a sort of strength from them—the strength, I think, of knowing he was part of the earth no matter how excluded and rejected by the rest of humanity. (He went to good lengths to give the rest of humanity cause to reject him at times.) He belonged to the earth as much as anyone and in that found defiance and strength and a kind of companionship against meaninglessness.

Feb. 13th

I woke, done sleeping before dawn. The eastern sky was just beginning to lighten so I lay still and watched it change to lighter and lighter shades of violet. The stars stayed bright. Then the sky was light, white light. After a while, a red sunrise came up but not before this interlude of pale, white light. It often seems like that in the morning—beautiful dawn, then nothing, then a beautiful sunrise. Louis woke just before sunrise and we hiked to the two small hills to the west of the truck and watched the sun come up.

On a glorious plain of amber grass north of Marathon, Texas, we pulled to the roadside and made breakfast. The jacks were excellent because the sourdough batter has been in the back of the truck for three days. I made it on the banks of the Llano River.

The mountains closed in as we approached Big Bend National Park. When we entered the park, it

North of Marathon, Texas

seemed to me that the desert plants almost doubled in number. Prickly pear in particular seemed more numerous, and instead of seeming barren the desert here seems bountiful. Is this the result of taking cattle off the range?

We decided to hike into the Chisos Mountains. Saw two very tame whitetail bucks on the way in. Whitetails moved into these mountains during the last Ice Age, when things were cooler, and now they can't escape because the surrounding desert is too harsh and dry for them.

This place has the wonderful spicy aroma of the desert. I think it is sage and maybe creosote bush. Below, the hills fall into deep ravines almost magical in steepness. On the mountainside, the evening sun plays a thousand games on the desert plants. Nowhere but in the desert are there so many angles for the sun, all spread out like a low palette—lobed prickly pear, saw-toothed yucca, and savagely sharp century plants, bunches of golden grass, and peaceful, green junipers. We are camped in a mountain desert paradise.

Feb. 14th

Woke at dawn and walked out to spot for cougars. Saw none. Arrived back at camp after three and a half miles, tired, dizzy, and hungry. Lentils and rice

Louis makes camp

Ravine south of our campsite

for breakfast, added the onion and extra water, oh goody.

We hiked down into the Blue Creek Canyon, enormous elevation loss. Explored a cave high on the hillside. Opening maybe 70 feet tall and 200 feet deep. What looks like smoke on the back wall. Did the first Americans camp here?

The hike back to camp was a push, although not as bad as we expected. I smell surprisingly like a hot horse and I don't get close enough to Louis to find out what he smells like.

I think the feeling of a canteen bottle on swollen, dry lips must be one of life's great simple sensations.

Walked out after supper to a low peak and lay looking up at the stars. Bit of a moon out for a few hours. Invented a few constellations and walked back by moonlight. Lots of wind right at dusk, but it is so still now that I can write by candlelight. I am writing from a very comfortable perch in an oak tree above the camp.

What a different perspective on life cougars must have. They have no tools or possessions to carry. Wherever they go they have all they need. No way to get lost if you have nothing to get lost from.

Feb. 15th

Passed a couple of women on the trail on our way out but were too dirty to feel like making any conversation. Washed my face in the fetid horse trough at Boot Spring and Louis discovered some sweet and ripe prickly pear fruit. He swallows the seeds. "Sure, man, spread the species," he says, and it takes me a minute to get it.

Made it to the top of Emory Peak, elev. 7,825 feet, and sat for a long time taking in the view. I wish we had come up here first because the whole mountain range is visible and we can see that hiking the east side would have been much more likely to produce a cougar sighting than the dry canyon we went into.

The women we passed earlier caught up to us. They are from New Orleans. Today is Mardi Gras day. Now we have justification from native New Orleanians that going west is the thing to do. We left shortly after they got to the peak; still, it was nice to talk with someone besides ourselves.

We drove around the western side of the park and in on a dirt road. Supposedly, you are only allowed down this road with a four-wheel drive, but we have no fear in the Long Bed. Our campsite is great; Louis picked it off the map. Overlooks the river, although a thick plain of tangled trees, most of which sport unforgiving thorns, blocks access to the water. We drove another five or six miles in and found a place we could wash our pots. The Rio

Grande smells like a sewer. I had planned to bathe, maybe swim to Mexico, but I don't want to get wet in this scum.

The border fascinates me. It is so prominent on maps and marks such a ravine between people's lives, but here it is nothing. Same dirt over there as right here. You can throw a stone across.

Louis saw a coyote walking after dark but he couldn't find any scorpions.

Feb. 16th

I woke just at dawn and was glad to get up and out. Woke Louis but he didn't seem to want to go, although he didn't respond directly, just muttered something about how it sounded as though I was throwing ball bearings into the truck. I was sorry that he didn't want to go but when I saw that he wasn't, I hustled out, hoping he wouldn't change his mind and make me wait while he looked for his socks.

When Louis woke, we walked out into the canyon we could see from the truck. I felt some sort of tension between us, or perhaps he is just depressed. Anyway, we rolled some large boulders of pumice off the cliff top and watched them crash into the canyon bottom 80 feet below and it perked up our spirits considerably. Nothing like destruction to bring people together and instill camaraderie.

Set out around 11:00 and fairly shortly came to a boat launch at the Santa Elena Canyon. We stood for a long time in the cold water. It smelled a good deal cleaner than downstream. Finally, I went in and found that the bottom, which was silty and muddy near the shore, improved greatly a few feet in. We waded against the current to Mexico. Water about up to our chests at the deepest but a good flow. We would have ended up well downstream if we had swum it. Bottom was stony and the water good and cold. No different on the Mexican side. We felt somewhat cleaner—cleaner of our own dirt, anyway.

Headed north up until we came to Guadalupe Mountains National Park and slipped in unannounced to the camping area. Hope we can slip out tomorrow. We are taking nothing and leaving nothing so they shouldn't mind.

Feb. 17th

Made it into Carlsbad Caverns National Park about an hour before they opened the cave. We pulled to the distant end of the parking lot and commenced jack making. Ate them with syrup and occasionally peanut butter. Halfway through our meal, the Ranger Dick cop car approached and slowed menacingly beside us. We expected a "We're sorry, gentlemen, there's no cooking or camping in the parking lot."

Instead, a folded-faced ranger, obviously a friendly, curmudgeonly type, rolled down his window. "There's a picnic table right under those trees there, if you'd like to use it."

You can enter Carlsbad either by the natural entrance or drop down by elevator. The natural entrance is a great sink in the ground not dissimilar from Weybridge Cave but much bigger. Steep, switchback ramps descend. The cave is made of limestone, or the absence of limestone in what would otherwise be a solid plate of limestone 2,000 feet thick, which formed as a reef from the calcified bodies of trillions of ancient sea creatures. Then the ocean departed and the ground under the reef uplifted. Moisture and water-soluble acids widened and enlarged the cracks and fissures, slowly making enormous cavities, which then, once formed, collapsed at the natural entrance, exposing everything to the air, which more or less stopped the enlargement.

The cave exceeds fanciful imaginations of caves. Great shelves, towering ceilings, tiny, impossible-looking passageways, a maze of interconnecting and disappearing passageways, and all in dust-covered gray limestone, etched and hollowed into fancifully bubbly masses. There are icicles going up and down, little pools of clear water, and rubble fallen from the ceiling eons ago but still not so long ago as to put us entirely at ease.

We passed through on the paved walkways, looking down into the depths, sometimes seeing figures 80 or 110 feet below us. All in all we dropped 750 feet. Louis was in awe and staring transfixed at the soaring ceilings and, as always, catching little curiosities, small nooks, or oddly colored rocks while processions of retirees and maybe even geriatrics passed by us.

The cave is huge, with wings and corridors spreading in all directions, many of which are unexplored. It seems the silent womb of creation, the immobile, monochromatic source of inchoate matter. It is, of course, just an ancient reef on which long-forgotten sunlight played, dappling the shallow waters while fish lolled lazily along shelves and tropical plants flourished nearby. It has been submerged, covered, uplifted, buried, aged, and recycled by the earth.

We walked past holes dropping into the lower cave, past huge formations rising slowly out of the cave floor, formed by water dripping from the ceiling. Water percolating through the ground above takes six or eight months to make its way from clouds to cave.

I kept thinking how the cave reminded me of the human mind—passageways after passageways, all connected, all covered in a confusing array of little nooks and caves, some dead ends, some leading to others, some circling around, underlaid with still more caves and maybe even undiscovered or unused rooms or passageways and perhaps even easier but unknown entrances.

Lunch today featured a near meltdown. We settled on using the falafel mix we have had since Vermont and I got confused over the directions, which called for cold water, although I thought it needed hot until Louis corrected me. Then we disagreed on how to cook it. Louis wanted to form patties, as the directions said, and fry them in oil. I, having tried patties with similar stuff at Enchanted Rock, knew that it just got your fingers messy as hell and thought we could just pour some oil in, stir it around, and eat gruel.

For some reason, it became incredibly important whose method we used. And then it became more important to use the other one's method to prove that we were flexible and that it wasn't a big deal. I was livid and can only assume that Louis was also. I remember thinking how odd it was to be so mad, furious that Louis was pissed at me for wanting to do it my way. Eventually, we gruel-cooked them, it tasted terrible, and we decided that one person ought to have final say over each meal.

※

Camped on the range. Long, fruitless, and bitter discussion over the fight over falafel and generally how we decide what we do. Louis feels that we do everything my way, but also that in general he has been satisfied with the trip or has not missed anything he wanted to see or done anything he didn't want to do. I agree about the last but feel trapped. I can't say directly what I want or don't want or else it becomes law by virtue of seniority so I hedge, which makes Louis mad.

Louis made home fries for supper, one of the best meals so far.

Feb. 18th

Mad-dog coyote yowls at dawn. Very misty and foggy this morning, but it burned off by the time we were ready to dust, around 8:30. Jacks for breakfast again.

Went to the federal building and got a map of Lincoln National Forest. Another guy was there buying a permit to take rock out of the national forest, $10 for four tons. He had lived in western Pennsylvania and said he missed it, but he also pointed out that Pennsylvania has 10 times as many people as New Mexico and New Mexico has three times as much land, although maybe not three times as much water. We agreed that there were too many people in the East and got an appreciative nod from the forest service man.

We headed out to the "rim" of the Guadalupe Mountains on Forest Service Road 540, a solid gravel road. Wind at the rim was truly amazing. Enough to rock the Long Bed as though someone was standing up and down on the bumper. The rim looks out from perhaps 2,000 feet above the plains and foothills of New Mexico. It is an escarpment, magnificent and fully worthy of such a nice word.

Feb.19th

Woke several times in the night dreaming that someone was shaking the truck and roused to find that it was only the wind. Some sort of comfort surrounds being buffeted but immune from the storm.

We set out around 8:00 and decided to follow 137 and turn off onto dirt roads toward Pinon, New Mexico. We had half a tank of gas and several gallons of water, so it seemed like a feasible plan, especially since the forest service map covered most of the terrain and even Rand McNally showed connecting roads. Where Rand McNally shows roads, anyone can go. By the end of the day that theory held true, but just barely.

Louis leans into the wind at the edge of the escarpment

The roads were rough, with inch-and-a-half or two-inch gravel, fine for a semi or even a big Ford but rough on small, 14-inch Japanese rims. We were held to 15 or 20 miles an hour for all but short, smooth stretches of the trip. Perhaps we covered 60 miles, give or take 10 or 20; we neglected to check the odometer. We stopped along the road to make breakfast and shortly after that came to an intersection where one road turned off to Dell City, Texas, and the other to Pinon. The road to Dell City had been noted several times by signs, but this was the only sign we saw to Pinon. Let it be said that both roads seemed equally well traveled and we took the one to Pinon.

So far, we had passed two trucks, and those were all we saw until we got to Pinon around 2:00. Once we made a wrong turn, but after two or three miles, Louis, who was navigating, caught the mistake. We backtracked and saw the windmill, which was the only available landmark for the intersection, and turned right instead of left.
So it was for the rest of the trip. Louis navigated by vague landmarks, windmills, water tanks, and, eventually, a pipeline that crossed and recrossed the road and also showed up on the forest service map. After 1:00 we started passing ranches, often deserted looking, every five or six miles, but before that there was a stretch where a breakdown or

Windmill landmark

wrong turn might have meant a long walk or several days' wait for help.

To our right, the escarpment rose for nearly the whole day. As we got to Pinon, the range land grew noticeably more grassy and pretty, with small rounded hills dotted by junipers and brown grass blowing over in the wind. Beyond Pinon, we climbed into the mountains past the town of Weed and toward the ski village of Cloudcroft. Here we saw small, plowed plots, some traces of snow along the north facing banks, water in small streams, and several orchards, both plum and apple.

Descending down the other side of the mountains, we came into the desert again and were sorry to leave what felt like a much more permanent and habitable place. Camped at White Sands.

We hiked around a bit in the moonlight. The bright light on the white sand reminded me of pictures I have seen of Arabs in the Empty Quarter [of Saudi Arabia] and I said as much to Louis, which started him on a discourse about the Burke and Wills expedition across Australia. They thought it was beautiful while they were still in the dunes, but then they got to the rocks. Eventually, both of them died and only one of the four-member party made it back. "Fucked up for the rest of his life," according to Louis.

But then, they did stupid things, like marching during the heat of the day. Louis and I walked out at night, confident we could follow our tracks back, and we did, but with enough difficulty to make us happy that we didn't go any further than we did. Slept on the beautiful white sand under the moon.

Feb. 20th

Day began at dawn with a discussion of whether or not to rise before the sun reached our sleeping bags. Decided to wait and then debated what was meant by "reached the sleeping bags"—just to the tops or all the way down? Argument waked us sufficiently to rise and spar with our sticks. Packed quickly and shuffled to the truck over the cold sand. Some ice in the water bottles.

Louis did not believe that there is a waffle and pancake house in every town, but we found one sure enough in Alamogordo, and stopped for breakfast, only the second time we have treated ourselves to restaurant food since leaving Vermont. A cheerful lad greeted us and had us sitting at the counter before we even knew what was happening.

Louis impressed the waitress by ordering a double load of pancakes (six), finishing them despite her doubts, and downing three more as well. Some mention was made of how much more perfectly cooked they were than our own variety and also how long we had been camping. "We were all looking at you and saying, 'Look at their hair,'" confided the boy who had seated us. I guess it is pretty stiff.

Stopped for gas in Carrizozo and were witness to an exciting incident. I heard it from the bathroom but missed seeing the action. We had just crossed Route 380 and were parked in the northeast corner of the intersection. Simultaneously, an old man walked toward Louis to say hello and Louis saw some cops speeding east on 380 toward the intersection. "Must be going to get coffee," said the old guy to Louis.

"Yeah," replied Louis, "doughnut sale."

"Those law dogs are crazy around here," returned the old guy.

Then a brown truck made a squealing corner through the parking lot right in front of Louis. The truck had been in front of the cops, but the cops cut them off on the corner and they ended up going through the parking lot, three very ashen- faced Mexicans with droopy mustaches in a tan pickup. They flew out of the parking lot and onto a dirt road that, fortunately, happened to be there, crossing the railroad tracks and catching air as they went over.

The cops, who had successfully negotiated the turn onto 54, were separated from the dirt road and unable to get it, so they pulled over and got out of their car. They were joined by a Blazer full of more cops, and together they watched the Mexicans disappear into the desert.

We stopped at Gran Quivira, site of an ancient pueblo and then a mission. The first missionaries arrived just before the 17th century, Christian time, and began converting the Indians, infecting them with diseases, and demanding tribute for their Spanish king and church. The Indians already had a method of worship which they carried on in round sub-terranean pits walled with stone.

The monstrous influence of our minds over our actions seems especially stark when one gazes out over the plains surrounding Gran Quivira and then onto the round kivas, where the Indians worshipped, and back to the enormous mission church that sits almost on top of the pueblo.

Here one person's beliefs about the unknown collided with a different belief, and the differences are set in stone—the round and buried version vs. the cross-shaped and raised. Which is better is an open and possibly foolish question, although one of life and death to the participants.

Eventually, the two managed to somewhat coexist—not, of course, until disease had decimated the Indians and the pueblo revolt had diminished the Christians. Now there is nothing but the stone markers.

> *'My name is Ozymandias, king of kings;*
> *Look on my works, ye Mighty, and despair!'*
> *Nothing beside remains. Round the decay*
> *Of that colossal wreck, boundless and bare*
> *The lone and level sands stretch far away.*

Shelley—"Ozymandias"

Got to Santa Fe in the afternoon. We have landed in paradise for travelers—Herb's splendid, luxurious, and generous quarters. [Herb was the leader of the St. John's College Search and Rescue team when I was a student there and for years after.]

Feb. 21st

Visited St. John's College and got Louis an appointment to sit in on some classes on Thursday.

Climbed Monte Sol and Monte Luna with Louis. Had an enormous supper with Herb, Dr. Allen, and many others. We are living amidst opulence, basking in its reassurance, unfettered by its responsibility.

Feb. 22nd

After lunch, we climbed Atalaya. Nasty climb with ice under snow, but clouds parted and we got a beautiful Santa Fe view, dark clouds fading into a brightening sky.

Feb. 23rd

Baked a batch of sourdough that I started last night and it turned out well despite the altitude. Louis and I polished off nearly an entire loaf of hot bread between us. Herb was rather shocked by our gluttony.

It was a day of experiences with the free market system. We stopped at a health food store called Wild Oats, notoriously expensive, according to Herb, and I don't doubt that he is right if you are buying prepacked, yuppie health-food delights.

We settled for organic flour, whole wheat, 39¢ a pound. Earlier, we had priced flour at the giant Furrs Supermarket and found some whole wheat organic at five pounds for $3.99. Actually, we would have settled for regular whole wheat, pesticides and all, but the only brand at Furrs besides the high-priced organic was a brand we had bought in Mississippi and found bitter. So we held out for the health food store and were rewarded with 39¢ organic flour.

We also stopped at the used paperback bookstore and, after some deliberation, walked out with a book of collected poetry, three of economist John Kenneth Galbraith's best efforts, *Murder on the Orient Express*, two Louis L'Amours, and short stories of Poe, for $4.83. The selling price was 40 percent of the cover prices.

Maybe Thoreau would have a pompous comment about old knowledge being less valuable than new knowledge even though the words are the same. Apparently, the free market has determined that one 1967 copy of *The New Industrial State* (1.24 x .4) equals 1.3 pounds of organic flour or one Snickers bar or a cup of coffee. There is something wonderful here and also something wrong.

The bread baking today raised the question of baking while camping and reminded Herb of his reflective oven and aluminum shield that fits over the baking tray and directs the heat from a campfire onto whatever is in the tray. In his early days in Outward Bound, they used these all the time. We uncovered his old oven, a conveniently designed model that folded into a dust-covered green bag. Eventually, he located a new model in his outdoor catalogs and we will order one.

Herb also brought out his old camping and woodcraft books, the type that many American children grew up fascinated by. Herb has the best selection not only in volume but also quality that I have ever laid eyes on—books with frail, brittle pages and crude, manly diagrams, sometimes not even crude but sensitive in the clumsy sort of way of someone who understands the subtleties but is too unrefined to produce them. Stories and instruction for how any true American with a little common sense, perseverance, and toughness could go into the woods and live not too different from ol' Dan'l Boone—independent, self-reliant, close to the land. The reassuring American notion that given a bit of wilderness and some courage, anyone could make a place for them-selves in the world.

Feb. 24th

Took Louis to St. John's for a day of classes and propaganda. A bunch of assholes talking about bullshit is how he described it.

Feb. 25th

Morning started bright with anger. The night before, I had mentioned that there would be a lot to do the next day to get ready and so I was mildly miffed when Louis slept in. But when I discovered that not only was he sleeping late but that he was actually lying in bed reading, it pissed me off. Eventually, we worked together cleaning and repacking the truck. I was trying to be friendly, since I didn't know what to do about my anger and couldn't decide if it was justified.

Louis noticed my silence and asked me if something was wrong. I acknowledged that it pissed me off to have him reading while I was doing our work but that I didn't know what to do about it. We finished the truck in awkward silence. I felt happy relief of having gotten it off my chest and refrained from saying anything else. Louis said nothing either.

We shoved off for Albuquerque around 3:00. Got to Seth's place a little after 4:00. He had been waiting for us and popped out of his cave-like adobe house to greet us. His house is small but surprisingly comfortable, strewn with artifacts from his travels— small bronze figurines of elephants and mummies, a tapestry from an Afghanistan tent, a tea kettle with the handle and spout on the same side.

As Seth pointed out, he is still trying to get into medical school, as he was talking about doing when we were both freshmen at St. John's, and I am still talking about buying a piece of land. Neither of us is appreciably closer to these achievements, although he has put a great deal more effort toward his. He treated us to Thai food and then we walked around the bleak campus of UNM, back to his place, and talked until 3:00.

Feb. 26th

Seth woke at 6:30 after three and a half hours of sleep and stumbled out to his day of work with psychotic children. I managed some sort of sleepy goodbye from my bag. By 6:45 Louis was up and loading the truck. Didn't even notice the Rio Grande as we passed through Albuquerque and over it out into the dry plains west of Albuquerque.

We took 117 just before Grants, N.M., and headed off through some prettier country with cliffs shaped in inviting curves and a few green junipers sprinkled about. I think one major distinction between different types of land is whether it was shaped by life or geology. In the West, the land shapes result from uplifts, ancient volcanoes, and erosion. The beds of departed seas rise in sections along the roadside, and every mountain and cliff is gracefully skirted with debris that has sloughed off its walls and piled along its base. Plants and animals hold and make their places against these forms of geologic creation.

In the East, by contrast, the plants have so covered and clothed the landscape that their shapes and creations are the primary cause of what we see—rounded hills, hillocks raised by trees, ponds and plains leveled by beavers—and it all makes for a very different feel to the landscape.

Then too one is always aware of the incredible, literally incredible, passage of time so that the West, where now bony structures push up from the earth, there was once a tropical shore surrounded by a warm, shallow tropical sea with a disgusting growth of vegetation and fish and mud and giant ferns all spreading under a thick, wet sky. So where the landscape now seems defined by geology, it was covered in plants that have passed by and become geology again.

To this story also must be added the shape humans put on the land, shapes that are both the most beautiful (at least to humans) and the most hideous.

Drove on toward Silver City and past the beautiful, rough-looking Mogollon Mountains, passing over the Continental Divide several times. Some farming through here in fertile-looking valleys. Got to Jenny Ruskey's [John's sister] house around 6:00 and were treated to a delicious supper.

Feb. 27th

Jenny needed a low rock wall built in her yard so she could flatten and terrace the yard for flower gardens. We drove into the Gila National Forest, collected pretty stones from the road cut, and spent most of the day making the wall. The stones have copper in them and are prettily flecked with green and red.

Jenny found a black widow spider while we were collecting rocks. Despite its reputation, it curled into a defenseless ball under our prodding with grass stems. Vivid hourglass shape and shiny black.

On the last load of rocks, the Long Bed had a flat tire on the front. We changed with our lumpy spare but will have to get the tire fixed tomorrow.

Our wall was neither pretty nor stable and as Vermonters we felt ashamed, but out here there is no frost to topple it. The day spent making something was extremely satisfying and enjoyable. It throws the road trip somewhat into doubt. We are both saturated with observation and would like to be making things. It must be worse for Louis. At least I am making the journal.

Louis discovered ant mimics while we worked on the wall — small bugs designed to look like ants as protection from ants. He had only read about them until now and is pleased.

Feb. 28th

At breakfast, Jenny told us about the time she interviewed some old Hispanic people and they talked about what it was like to go to public school in Silver City in the 1950s. Many of them spoke no language other than Spanish when they first went to school, and at school they were punished with a ruler for talking in Spanish, so their only language became a source of pain and embarrassment for them. And yet, according to Jenny, they said that they didn't tell their children about it because they didn't want their children to hate the Anglos.

Here is a sad irony. Once the Hispanic people were punished for speaking the language of their parents, and now they are taught in Spanish and may not even learn English and so will become either second-class citizens in their country or rebels, unable to fit into America.

Left our tire off to be fixed and headed up to Gary and Lou Ruskey's house. [Lou Ruskey is John's mother and Gary is her husband.] Gary and Lou have made great progress turning their piece of desert into an oasis, helped, of course, with water piped up by the town. Setting aside the water question, the place is a testament to perseverance and dedication to doing what they can when they can.

Gary doesn't pass a small wash without pausing to toss some stones in. Consequently, there are small dams everywhere, some of which have two or more feet of what would have been erosion piled up behind them. I hesitate to call the collection behind the dams "dirt" because it isn't in an ordinary sense. Mostly the ground is made of decomposed pink granite and sand, and under the surface—sometimes on the surface—is granite bedrock. It is, despite the harshness, a delicate environment but one which responds to care.

They have planted pecans, almonds, plums, apples, apricots, grapes, flower gardens, and a vegetable garden. Little mounds of dirt circle each tree and mats of straw protect their feet from evaporation.

Boarded Interstate 10 in Lordsburg and rolled west with the other license plates. Just beyond the second exit for the road to Safford, Arizona, we saw the most unusual interstate traveler yet, going east in the other lane. It was a man on a cart behind a horse. We took the next exit five or six miles up the road, reversed direction, and caught him. I thought as we passed that he might be black, but we saw that he was just weathered—a brown white man, full beard and black hat.

Don Boyer, his horse, and his dog, who gave me a hell of a static shock when I reached out to pat him. Since there was no frontage road, the police didn't hassle him about his horse on the interstate.

The horse was only two. Don was breaking him in and said he had more trouble keeping him from shying at spent truck tires and at his hat when it flies off his head than at the passing trucks.

They made about 20 miles a day, hauling Don's camping equipment and food for the two of them and about 25 gallons of water. He'd been on the road for about six months this time, spending around $50 a week and making money selling the leatherwork and jewelry he makes. Usually, he travels in a four-wheel wagon with his entire shop inside.

"You ever get to missing people out here like this?" I asked.

"Naw, anywhere you can go in this rig there are people. There are people everywhere. Now, I could go up there in the desert, if I wanted to put a saddle on him, and get way out, not see anyone. Where are you headed next?"

"Well, I guess we are headed toward LA."

"Yuck, too many people out there."

"I know what you mean."

"I was raised out there in that country. That's pretty country, but they ruined it. You like the desert country?"

"Yeah, I do. Guess I'm more of a woodsman, though," I said.

"Well, you see, if you're raised in it like I was, then you get where there are trees and it's just like fences all around you."

His shoes were new and even clean—actually, all his clothes were, although his hands showed the same dusty dirt ours do after several days of conserving water. We left him with one mile to go before he pulled off at the Safford exit.

We drove into the Sonoran Desert, leaving behind the yellow, brushy desert near Silver City and entering the green Sonoran full of cacti and thorns, lower and rockier—the land of the saguaro cacti standing like friendly figures on all the hillsides.

Stopped at the Biosphere 2 to make a phone call. It sits beside beautiful mountains and overlooking a pretty canyon. It is remarkably small in the expanse of desert, remarkably ugly by comparison too. Since the real trouble is controlling ourselves, I don't see how a world full of biospheres will save us from the problems we have created. We already live in a terrarium; it's just 25,000 miles around instead of four acres like the Biosphere.

Another piece of American freedom fell to increasing social breakdown. Now law-abiding people must wait five days before buying a handgun.

March 1994

March 1st

Slept without incident. How many nights now have we gone to sleep unsure of our spot? Would some rancher throw us off, would some criminal assault us, would some animal object to our presence? And how many nights have passed uneventfully?

Louis slept in, and I walked before sunrise. Beautiful country, mostly treeless but watched over by hundreds of saguaro and other succulents. They give a gentle green cast to everything. Beyond where we parked, I found an old mine entrance, just a dark cavity in the mountain, and then another and another farther up the hillside.

Louis woke feeling sick. Ate dry granola for breakfast and not much. We walked out to explore the mines. We could almost walk upright in the first mine, but a swarm of flies that we mistook for bees repulsed us at first. Finally, Louis deduced that if they had been bees they would have already stung us, and he caught one against the mine wall with his light and confirmed the identification.

It was strangely warm inside the mine, perhaps from yesterday's heat, and maybe that is what attracted the flies.

The mine proved only 100 feet deep or so, neatly cut into the rock mountain. It must have been a hell of a job, backbreaking and dangerous.

The next shaft was larger, contained several passageways, including two vertical ones that were full of water. We could not see the bottom nor see a rock make its way all the way there, but it had been pumped at one time.

The third mine was more of a cave, higher up on the opposite mountain slope and in softer rock. We had to crawl to enter and inside found pieces of collapsed ceiling. "Let's leave," Louis said, and then he spotted an intersecting vein of rock and we both returned to examine it. Who knows, perhaps the collapsing ceiling had exposed the sought-for ribbon of gold and we were the lucky finders.

The mines are peculiar curiosities, empty pits, really, but everyone hopes—and we hoped too in some small way—that poking just the right hole in Old Mother Earth and perhaps she would reward us with, what? What was it those old miners wanted so much? Wealth? And what's that? Security? So they dug, living and working in the most dangerous circumstances, hoping that a lucky thrust would free them from worry and danger forever.

Louis at the wheel

Drove on and on into the Arizona hills and mountains, eventually climbing to where there was snow and a forest of large trees. I relaxed immediately among the trees and had not realized how much I missed them. Beautiful country in the setting sun, with the mountains silhouetted and the sky winter-yellow pale. Louis said that it reminded him strongly of Alaska. Saw a coyote crossing the road.

Planned to treat ourselves to a campground since one showed on the map just south of Flagstaff, but it was closed and the next closed also. Made a long drive south after dark to Dead Horse Ranch State Park Campground. Lost lots of altitude and we can't tell what sort of territory we are in, but we did get hot showers.

March 2nd

Paid our $10 and eventually got a permit to hike Kaibab Trail to Bright Angel Campground at the bottom of the Grand Canyon. A man on the trailhead said to us, "If you see that old girl laid out down there, haul her back up here for me, would ya?" I guess they had a fight and this was his way of making light of it. She was out of sight several hundred yards down, crying be-hind her oversized glasses.

The hike down was quick, no more than three hours. We'll see about tomorrow. Sweet and sour mule shit all the way down. Lots of hikers too, despite the ranger's assurances that there wouldn't be. Most of the hikers smell like perfume or soap or toothpaste. I'm surprised at how strong it is.

Anasazi pueblo at the bottom of the canyon. We are sleeping on what used to be corn, bean, and squash plots. The weather changed about 1150 AD and they left. I looked hard at the stonework of the buildings, low down, below where the park service touched it up, and tried to imagine what sort of person laid it up, but I couldn't tell. Less predisposed to the angular and rectilinear than the park service, but not much else.

I'm not a canyon person, even though it is beautiful here, and the desperately green color of the willows, light but vivid and translucent, like flags of paradise. Still, I feel closed in, maybe like Don Boyer feels in a forest. We took a quick swim in the Colorado. Mighty cold. Our skin felt punctured and our legs ached.

March 3rd

Slept under bright stars and woke to see the moon chasing them away through the narrow fold of sky visible between the canyon walls. The moonlight was so bright Louis couldn't sleep and got up to walk around. He tried reading by moonlight but found it slightly too dim. Woke again to find the sun chasing the moon away.

Must have left around 10:30 and felt good and strong. We passed tons of people and the river fell away very rapidly. After a couple of miles, we caught up with the mule team and passed them too and pushed on feeling very good.

The trail is switch-backed so as to be a fairly easy incline considering what it ascends. Our egos took small gulps of satisfaction every time we blew by another puffing hiker.

We were passed only twice, both times by women. The first must have started out later than us and overtook us about halfway along. She wasn't carrying much but still we watched her disappear with some dismay.

At the sign marking 1.5 miles from the top we hit the wall. We ate some and pushed on, but we had nothing left to feed our legs except pain. Every couple of hundred yards our legs would simply go weak and pushing on was excruciating. A short rest of maybe two minutes and we felt better, but it didn't last. Neither of us was out of breath and we had drunk plenty of water, but our legs had nothing left to give.

The mule skinner passed us when we stopped to try eating. "I thought you guys would be at the top," he said in a snide, shit-eating voice.

We passed him again, resting his mules, too fucking lazy to haul his ass out of the saddle and give the lead mule a proper rest. But he caught us again, half a mile or so farther on. "You guys always go too fast. It always kills you right about here," he said as he passed. The prick obviously took great satisfaction in his trifling wisdom and experience.

I spent the rest of the climb silently hoping he would overwork his mules and one of them would drop him over the edge. He must have beaten us by 10 or 15 minutes to the top because the mules weren't even unloaded when we got there.

We were passed once more, about eight switchbacks from the top, by a woman who had passed our camp about 8:00 that morning. We overtook her quite early on the climb, but she came piling by us, ski poles for walking sticks, and there was nothing we could do to catch up. Chalk up a mark for feminine endurance.

Still, we made it to the top in about three and a half hours, only one of which was painful. The climb proved a hell of a lot easier than we expected.

A big hiker walked by us as we unpacked.

"You beat those mules?"

"Nope. The ranger was kind of an asshole about it too."

"Yeah, they're good at that. You guys were motoring when you passed me."

"We burned out shortly after that."

"Me too, man."

The guy had the build that makes for a tough hiker, large boned and muscled, a little flabby, the sort that can go all day long, days in a row carrying a heavy pack, which he was—a condominium, as he called it—and it held hip waders.

We talked about John McPhee. He had read, *Coming into the Country*, *Basin and Range*, *Encounters with the Archdruid*, and *The Control of Nature*. He told us of a hike he did in the canyon with several other people when there was an earthquake. "I felt a hell of a lot safer down there than I would have in town."

"Yeah, unless the dam lets loose."

"Wouldn't that be a shame."

"Yeah."

"You read Edward Abbey?"

"Yeah, we've got it in the back of the truck right now," Louis said.

"*The Fool's Progress*, that's like a Bible, man," said the hiker.

"That's the one I brought," Louis said.

"Go to hell, Henry."

"Yeah, yeah."

We made for the forest service campground near Jacob Lake, 8,000 feet elevation, but it was closed. The poor Long Bed had to do almost as much climbing as we did today. It was almost out of gas when we passed Jacob Lake and the gas station was closed, so we pushed on for 10 miles and then blasted through seven or eight inches of snow onto a roadside turnout. We were too tired to cook.

March 4th

Slept badly. Probably the result of peanut butter and cheese supper. We got rolling fairly early and rolled right down the plateau and into the town of Fredonia without running out of gas. The gas station attendant noticed our missing battery cap, the one that fell off somewhere in New Mexico, and offered a replacement from some discarded batteries.

Is Utah different from Arizona in how people treat the land? And is it because the people are Mormons? Farms, small fields, and plowed land started almost as soon as we crossed the border. Perhaps the land here is more fertile or wetter and that accounts for the difference. It is hard to say.

Drove for most of the day north on 89 along the pretty Sevier River. Sometimes the mountains closed in too closely for there to be any fields, but where fields were possible it seemed as though somebody was maintaining them. We pulled off the road north of Panguitch and made some sandwiches for lunch, read, and I napped.

The farms kept increasing and we stopped in Palisades State Park. It was open but all the bathrooms were closed and there was no running water. Nevertheless, we got water free from an adjacent golf course. Small lake here and springtime birds.

March 5th

We made a pact to limit conversational flatulence. Things were getting out of hand, and causing something of a health hazard. Probably the result of too much peanut butter and cheese.

Heard a rooster crow this morning and hiked up a small mountain and saw several farms laid out in adjoining valleys. Stark land for farming but the

Mormons are having a go at it. We dusted along through more of the same sort of land—open valleys full of farms between mountains.

Passed through a number of small towns with houses uncharacteristic for the West, solid brick and two story, often hideous from any aesthetic point of view but obviously substantial and built to last. Almost as though a group of New Englanders had been instantly transplanted but stripped of any concept of architectural beauty. We stopped in several small groceries. The people here are sadistically friendly, even to us, dirty and out of place as we are.

We were interested to see if the farming in Utah would continue into the Nevada border, but after the town of Delta the desert took over and, apparently, even fervent Mormons were no match for it. We saw where the Sevier River, which had sustained such pretty farming valleys, flowed out into the sun and dried and died in an ugly, flat, empty lake.

We drove through basin and range—long flat valleys followed by mountain ranges. The land is being pulled apart here, according to John McPhee, and as it separates, the chunks tip slightly on the stew of molten rock beneath them, each break rising up or sinking down and making a mountain range.

It seems to be a plausible explanation to me, especially driving across it. I find it less than relaxing to drive across the hardened crust of earthly soup, especially since the pumice and volcanic-shaped mountains make it obvious that there is heat just beneath. All in all this terrain looks as though, were there only water, it might make a delightfully abundant landscape, fertile valleys neatly divided by mountains. Eventually, we pulled off the road and slept.

March 6th

We pushed out into the day, hoping for warmer weather before cooking breakfast. When we stopped to cook breakfast at a roadside picnic area, Louis cooked and I heard swears and shouts coming from behind the truck. The wind was steady and cool. He had to pour the oil several inches from the pot just so the wind would carry it in instead of spilling it.

The wind blew a pancake off Louis's plate and onto the gravel, although that didn't stop him from consuming it. I got a pat of margarine stuck on my fork. I shook the fork and tried to rub it off but couldn't because the grease sat safely inside the curve. In frustration, I gave a particularly quick snap of my wrist and the margarine flew off and landed squarely on the toe of Louis's boot. Fearing personal injury, I tried unsuccessfully to keep from laughing (even as I write this, it still rankles him). Louis scraped the margarine off with the spatula, the crudeness of which, he later confessed, surprised even himself. We rode on silently for several miles and reached our campsite at Wildrose in Death Valley, California around 2:00 and retired into the back of the truck to read.

March 7th

A day of long driving. We dusted fairly early, unwilling to make jacks in the wind and eager to get to Sequoia National Park and spend the afternoon reading. Followed the road to Isabella and there attempted a shortcut up to Johnsondale, following the canyon of the Kern River.

    We stopped by the river and I shaved and washed my face and hands and considered swimming, but the water seemed a bit murky, not to mention cold, so I skipped it and muttered something to Louis about the color of the water. He squinted at it disinterestedly and then squatted for a minute beside the bank. "Caddis flies," he pronounced, "a sign of very clean water," and strode off.

The road was blocked by snow so we backtracked all the way to Wolford, which cost us greatly both in time and reserve determination. In the space of several hours—four, maybe—we had gone from Death Valley to a snow-blocked pass in the Sierra Nevada, but the real surprise awaited us.

In Wolford, we boarded 155 for the over-the-mountain climb. It was a haul, second gear and rising into trees and snow, but as we descended the other side, miracles began to take place. The trees thickened noticeably at the top and grew denser for a way as we descended. Then, gradually, little patches of green grass began appearing, then whole glades and little meadows decorated with oaks. Behind us, we could still see the conifers and snow-filled ravines, but around us were tilled gardens, ferociously green, the first real green we'd seen since somewhere in east Texas.

> *So twice five miles of fertile ground*
> *With walls and towers were girdled round;*
> *And there were gardens bright with sinuous rills,*
> *Where blossomed many an incense bearing tree;*
> *And here were forests ancient as the hills,*
> *Enfolding sunny spots of greenery.*
>
>   *Coleridge—"Kubla Khan"*

We looked at each other, spellbound (is there another word?). Rounding a corner and seeing fold after fold of green hills sprinkled with rocks and trees, Louis dropped the map on his lap in utter astonishment. Down and down we wound through these inviting hills.

Eventually, we passed a few houses and then more hills, occasionally a fruit tree in bloom in front of a barn. Cows grazed on the slopes. "My God, the cow paths aren't even muddy. The cows don't even need hooves here," Louis said.

It was as though we had entered paradise, journeyed beyond the rest of the tired old world to one that was fresh and new.

Finally, we arrived in Glennville and a sign pointed us by the back road, unmarked on the map, to Porterville. Here was more of the same, paradise unpopulated, but as we approached Porterville the oaks and other trees thinned to make way for rolling hills covered in spring's gentle thatch of grass.

Then, on distant hills, Louis noticed rows of dark green trees, their lines marked out beautifully against the rising hillsides. Up close we passed through some. Oranges! And orange trees, their bright orange globes unmistakable in the waxy leaves, then lemons.

*
**

Our first attempt to steal the fruits of paradise almost ended in disaster. I reined the Long Bed to the roadside and immediately felt us slipping and sliding in the irrigated muck along the shoulder. If we'd stopped, we never would have gotten going. Fortunately, we had just enough momentum to regain the road, leaving incriminating streaks of mud behind us.

The next time, I parked politely beside the road while Louis helped us to two of California's finest.

We got lost in Porterville, a little town gone large, but found our way out and sped north on 65, experiencing the other side of paradise—paradise speeding by at 60 miles an hour with thousands of other rushed people. Still, the roadside stands were reminders—lemons, oranges, raisins, nuts, honey; we saw almond trees and grapevines.

What a joy California must have been to those who persevered. And what a curious lesson, onward and onward, as we have done on so many nights, knowing always that it was a mistake not to stop when we passed a good spot. But we kept pushing on, hoping to make a few more miles and then got stuck with nowhere good to sleep. And yet here, on a grand scale, the pushers and dissatisfied were rewarded for their discontent.

March 8th

We woke early and drove the winding road into the Sequoia Park's interior, passing through another version of paradise along the contours of the hills, past madrone trees and some beautiful flowers. Finally, we climbed high enough for large trees and then for really large trees, sequoias. Enormous trees are, to me at least, very relaxing.

We walked near the General Sherman Tree but did not immediately pick it out from the others and walked a little way into the woods before we came back to it. The largest living thing on earth, so they say: 275 feet tall, 1,385 tons, 36 feet across at the widest, and 2,300 to 2,700 years old. Neither the oldest nor the broadest, however, just the largest by virtue of rapid growth common to all sequoias.

It seems funny that longevity and enormous size should also combine with rapid growth. After 800 years, sequoias more or less stop growing up and concentrate on girth. This means that between the time of Jesus and the fall of the Roman Empire, this tree called it quits on height.

March 9th

Rolled out of the park into the heart of the valley. Paradise dimmed. Olive, almond, and orange trees falling away to miles of grapevines—thick, chunky, tortured stems crucified in rows miles long. Gradually, even the vineyards thinned out into fields of hay under a hazy sky. Eventually, we passed beyond even the farms of the valley and into a huge oilfield with lines of derricks almost as straight and numerous as the grapes.

There is yet something satisfying about seeing trucks of produce parked beside the road, rows of orderly crops. Satisfaction in seeing the economy at work rather than having to guess at what is produced in some shadowy building or trying to believe that the residents of some high-rise are adding meaningfully and usefully to our lives and the welfare of the country as a whole.

The question which must be addressed—it becomes obvious as one passes through California—is whether or not we are going to make a serious try at having the modern economy work or whether we need to revert to some possibly more primitive economy, but one also more peaceably disposed toward humans and the other lives in the world. Can we raise food like this and do it right? Is there a way to raise food on these enormously efficient farms, or is it simply too inhumane and too predicated on fossil fuels to be sustained?

※

We crossed the Sierra Madre and wound down toward the sea through another version of paradise and to the mighty 101 Highway and to Perry's house in Los Angeles.

March 10th

Woke early and enjoyed the quiet morning listening to the hurry of the city and reading. We took a fast ride in Perry's Mustang. The remarkable aspect of riding in a fast car driven by someone who knows how to drive is that all of your experiences and senses tell you that it is impossible to take the oncoming corner at the speed you are going, yet, with much tire squealing, you make it around just fine.

I think everyone has some aspect of their life, some experience or hobby or field of interest, in which they can truly be themselves and are able to overcome the problems they have in the rest of their life. For Perry, it is with cars and motorcycles that life makes sense; and also, that is where he finds analogies for how to live the rest of his life.

March 11th

Little enough to report today. Watched the morning news with Perry — the usual set of murders and drug deals. Perry is distraught about the loss of personal responsibility in this country. Sort of embodies the great American problem: a country founded on the individual and personal freedom, the frontier, democracy has somehow become the land where anyone's misfortune is someone else's fault. And in our money-measured society, that someone has to pay whatever can be extracted from them.

Jamie [Perry's wife] told us about the Northridge earthquake. She was thrown out of bed but made it into Hannah's room [their daughter, our cousin] and got her out of her crib. They stood together under the doorframe, watching the house move like a fun house at a carnival, everything at the wrong angles. All the lights went out and Jamie remembers seeing the crazy angles of the house in the moonlight which fell on as gentle and still as ever.

Epilogue

Adamant, Vermont, October 2017

We hung around with Perry for about a week and he took us back into the mountains surrounding Death Valley on jeep trails and unmarked gravel roads. Death Valley is Perry's favorite escape from LA. I found it inhospitable, beautiful, but slightly scary because it seemed so unearthly. Louis, less fearful and curious as always, was fascinated with the striations of different colored bedrock visible on some of the barren-looking mountainsides.

We stopped at Stella's cabin where a miner, Stella Anderson, lived by herself for years without car or electricity or running water or telephone. A person, an old person, alone in the vastness of the cosmos. At least that's how it felt to me standing next to her cabin high up the side of a desert mountain, as though you could fall off and tumble out into space. Surely it felt different to her. There were other lives there—the tough, scattered desert plants, wild burros and birds, human neighbors, even though they were miles distant, and friends and strangers passing by on the jeep trail who brought her supplies and took her to town occasionally.

A thin, precious miracle of topsoil and water, atmosphere, and the earth's magnetic field is all

In Death Valley with Perry

that sustains us on this planet. Death Valley felt to me like pictures of the moon or Mars—alien, dusty, timeless. And the buffer between life and the empty, uninhabitable stillness of space seemed especially small when we stood on a rocky slope near Stella's cabin and looked down into the dry valley far below.

For some desert dwellers, I think the scarcity of life is part of the attraction, keeping them ever mindful of its fragility. I get the same feeling when I see that unforgettable picture of a man floating weightless in space with our small, sapphire planet far away in the background. The man is encumbered by a space suit, as though in larval stage, and the planet is startlingly blue, unique in the infinity of darkness.

This image poses the question more elegantly than words ever can. Will we rise above nature, escape our terrestrial origins, and propagate ourselves throughout the universe? Or is that frighteningly small planet our future and our destiny?

Louis and I took a week to drive up the coast, mostly on US 1 from LA to Seattle. The spirit of the trip was gone. I gave up on the journal after LA, telling myself that I had completed a journal of our cross-country drive, which was true but it felt like a failure nonetheless.

We were just driving to get somewhere, which made it easier. I don't think we disagreed about anything on this part of the drive. After the Olympic Peninsula, we got on the interstate, burned up the miles, and got home to Vermont in late March.

I resumed woodworking, quite happy to be settled down and making things again. Perhaps there are two primary and conflicting forces inside people: to be settled and connected to a place, or to be free—roaming, observing, discovering. Those common ancestors who trekked out of Africa all the way to Australia and North America, what drove them? It is unlikely that it was overpopulation or scarcity of resources. It must be something in us, maybe the same thing in Louis and me—an instinct or maybe some sort of intrinsic discontent that tells us to see what is over the ridge.

The inimitable Jim Picone, whom I'd replaced as tenant in the house in Middlesex before the road trip, was now a homeowner himself and he became my new landlord. I fixed up an old sugarhouse on his property and lived in that for the summer before moving into his house for the winter.

I used Jim's basement as a woodshop for building furniture. Later that summer, an old welding shop about a mile from where Louis and I grew up came for sale at a very cheap price. The welding shop became my new woodshop and, eventually, house.

Beth Ann, who'd been my housemate, became my girlfriend, and two summers later we got married. We've raised two kids and still live in that now much retrofitted welding shop. I made furniture for 15 years and got thoroughly sick of it before several friends and I started a renewable energy business.

Louis eventually went to college, Arizona State in Tempe, where he studied ants for a couple of years before transferring to the University of Washington and graduating with a degree in zoology and another in history.

He worked on the college newspaper and got teargassed while covering the Battle for Seattle protests against the 1999 World Trade Organization meeting taking place in Seattle. This was so much fun that he embarked on a career in journalism, first in Connecticut and then back in Vermont. In 2014, he was appointed Fish and Wildlife Commissioner of Vermont, the youngest person ever to hold that position—a career, which, in retrospect, might have been predicted by his fascination with everything from scorpions to alligators and armadillos.

We live about half a mile apart now. Although he says he has forgiven me, our friendship never fully recovered from the falafel incident. Louis has become something of a foodie, perhaps partly as a defense against ever having to eat gruel-cooked falafel mix again. I still find peanut butter a satisfactory meal when necessary, much to the consternation of Beth Ann, who, like Louis, is an excellent cook.

I'm not sure what I was looking for on the road trip. I think I would have liked it if I had written a book and it had been published and that had started me off in a new direction. At the same time, when

I got home I was very satisfied to be woodworking and making things with my hands again.

I've been writing on and off since then. The journal writing that followed the cold, despairing evening at the Canaan Valley campground, where I decided to give up on writing a book and resolved just to write down the day's events, mostly as a defiance against completely giving up, taught me more about writing than anything else in my life.

What is clear, rereading my journal, is that I missed a lot of what was right in front of me. Every old man we met said some version of "Well, you got to do it when you're young."

A chance to drive across the country with your brother, every turn a new discovery, that's what I should have focused on. My worries about why I was keeping a journal or what I would do afterward or whether we should stop or make more miles, these weren't important.

I say that our friendship never recovered from the falafel incident but, in truth, it wasn't exactly a friendship. We were eldest and youngest siblings, and our relationship contained all of the baggage you'd expect—friendship and love, yes, but also hierarchy and misplaced admiration and expectations. It was probably inevitable that by the end of the trip, Louis would see me as less than he had at the beginning. I saw myself that way too. The factual brutality of your own limitations as a person is starkly exposed when you're living in the back of a truck.

We came home. Beth Ann and I have a family. Louis has a very successful career. The responsibilities and obligations are so many now that it is almost impossible to remember a time so carefree that we could just leave. But if I ever do it again, I'll try to keep in mind that the experience when you're having it is what is most important.

www.ingramcontent.com/pod-product-compliance
Lightning Source LLC
Chambersburg PA
CBHW050634300426
44112CB00012B/1793